TYING CLASSIC

Freshwater Streamers

TYING CLASSIC

Freshwater Streamers

AN ILLUSTRATED STEP-BY-STEP GUIDE

DAVID KLAUSMEYER

EDITOR, *FLY TYER* MAGAZINE

THE COUNTRYMAN PRESS
WOODSTOCK, VERMONT

ISBN 0-88150-596-X

Library of Congress Cataloging-in-Publication Data has been applied for.

Book design by Carol Jessop
Cover and interior photographs by the author

Published by The Countryman Press, P.O. Box 748, Woodstock, Vermont 05091

Distributed by W. W. Norton & Company, Inc., 500 Fifth Avenue, New York, NY 10010

Printed in Spain by Artes Graficas Toledo

10 9 8 7 6 5 4 3 2 1

Dedication

LAWRENCE LARGAY

This book is very different from the one I had originally planned. I'm happy with the final product, and I'll be so bold to say that I think it's a very good book. It teaches how to dress a variety of classic streamers and showcases the work of many important contemporary tiers. But it's different from what I first had in mind.

I was going to collaborate on this project with Larry Largay. Larry was the foremost fly-fishing and tying illustrator and photographer in the business. Together we produced *Tying Contemporary Saltwater Flies* (Countryman Press, 2002). That book received considerable praise in the angling press, and this would be a companion volume. Larry and I would work the same: I would write the text and take the fly-tying photographs, and he would produce fresh artwork and design the book—actually place the photos, art, and text on the pages. He would then send to the publisher a set of compact disks containing the completely finished book ready for the printer. Unfortunately, Larry suffered a fatal accident in January 2003. When I visited Larry's studio a couple of weeks later, I saw a to-do list he made the morning of the accident. Near the top was the line: "Start Streamer Book."

Larry said this would be his last book, but I doubted that. He lost track of the number of books he had illustrated and designed, but he wanted this one to be special. Larry was born and bred in Maine, the heart of freshwater streamer country, and this project was close to his heart. He was planning new watercolors of brook trout, landlocked salmon, and camping scenes, as well as a series of detailed schematics of classic guide boats. Larry's creativity and energy had no bounds.

Larry was a mentor and close friend. He became a beloved member of our family, and he will always remain close to our hearts. I dedicate this book to Lawrence Largay.

Contents

Introduction
Classics Never Go Out of Fashion ix

Chapter 1
The Anatomy of Classic Streamers 1

Chapter 2
Getting the Goods for Traditional Streamers 13

Chapter 3
Dressing the Classic Gray Ghost 23

Chapter 4
Upright Feather Wings: Dressing the Chief Needahbah 35

Chapter 5
Tying Tandem-Hook Streamers 41

Chapter 6
The Graduate Course: Tying the Lady Doctor 53

Chapter 7
Marabou Streamers: The Ballou Special 63

Chapter 8
Tying Bucktails: The Governor Aiken 69

Chapter 9
A Modern Classic: The Thunder Creek 75

Chapter 10
Everyone's Favorite: The Muddler Minnow 81

Chapter 11
A Gallery of Classic Streamers 87

Appendices
Purveyors of Streamer Materials 144
Bibliography 144
List of Featured Tiers: Great Streamer Dressers 145
Index 148

Introduction
CLASSICS NEVER GO OUT OF FASHION

When I was a boy growing up in the suburbs of Oklahoma City, I would ride my bicycle to a library near our home. It was a few miles away, but it was well worth the trip. I spent hours at that library, flipping through the pages of books about World War I airplanes, racing cars, and hunting.

One of the special treasures in that library was a small stash of books about fly fishing. An elderly gentleman had already shown me the wonders of using flies to catch bass and the rudiments of fly tying. I had attempted to tie a few flies, but my accomplishments were less than rudimentary. Solid information about dressing and fishing flies was extremely hard to come by back then—especially in the Oklahoma City suburbs—and these books opened a world of wonders and possibilities.

One of the books was Joseph Bates's *Streamers & Bucktails: The Big Fish Flies*. I devoured that book—over and over again. The beautiful patterns and the stories of the tiers captivated me: Carrie Stevens, Herbie Welch, Lew Oatman, Chief Neebahbah, and others. Oklahoma was (and probably still is) purple-plastic-worm country. There's nothing wrong with using plastic worms—I've used them to catch many fine fish—but I was drawn to the people in *Streamers & Bucktails*: it seemed as if they were living on another wonderful planet. Reading Bates inspired me to continue tying flies.

Classic freshwater streamers are as inspirational to fly tiers today as they were to me almost forty years ago. Whenever I write a magazine article about tying traditional streamers, I always receive letters from readers asking for more. And tiers specializing in dressing classic streamers are some of the main attractions at the today's fly-fishing shows.

Despite the interest in classic streamers, there are precious few books about them (you'll find the short list in the bibliography at the end of this book). All of the books I have read concentrate more on the personalities behind the flies rather than showing how to dress these marvelous patterns. I love all of those books—they occupy an important place in my library—but my goal with this volume is to show you how to tie the flies. Read those books to learn the stories behind the patterns; come here when you're ready to put a hook in the vise and start tying.

They say the classics never go out of style. This can certainly be said of classic freshwater streamers. These flies are still fascinating to study, beautiful to look at, challenging to tie, and they still catch fish. Classic streamers will never go out of fashion.

David Klausmeyer
Maine
Spring 2004

Chapter 1
THE ANATOMY OF CLASSIC STREAMERS

Some regional styles of fly tying and fishing have had profound influence on how we practice our sport. The dry flies developed in New York's Catskill Mountains—the Quill Gordon, Hendrickson, March Brown, Black Quill, and others—have influenced how we all tie and fish dry flies. Those patterns are the reference points on which all other dry flies are judged; we can identify new and innovative patterns based on those benchmarks.

The rivers of Montana, Idaho, and Wyoming are renowned for their hatches of large stoneflies. The anglers who fish those rivers have developed a host of patterns designed to imitate those insects. These flies, especially the large nymphs, are also some of the most deadly patterns for catching northeastern landlocked salmon. I've enjoyed memorable fishing using large nymphs that would be more at home on western rivers, and I'm meeting more anglers who are also experimenting with these patterns to catch trophy landlockeds.

New England, especially Maine's Rangeley Lakes region, has had a profound impact on the development of freshwater streamers. Hundreds of streamer patterns have been developed for catching trout and landlocked salmon. Most anglers identify feather-wing freshwater streamers, especially those having the full-feather wings mounted on the sides of the hooks, with New England. The same can be said of tandem-hook streamers designed for trolling, a time-honored early spring ritual for fishing lakes and ponds just after they shed their ice; what's called "ice-out" in the Northeast. Hair-wing streamers and bucktails, however, are more generic and not identified with

any specific region of the country. Still, most New England streamers have a common appearance identifying them with a separate school of fly tying.

I have always felt that Atlantic salmon flies had an influence on the development of classic feather-wing streamers. For many anglers from the Northeast, fishing for Atlantic salmon has always been just as important as, and certainly carries more of a mystique, than fishing for landlocked salmon and trout. Scores of Northeast fly fishermen have made annual pilgrimages to the famous Atlantic salmon rivers of New Brunswick, Quebec, Nova Scotia, and other Canadian provinces. Several Maine rivers also enjoyed a loyal following among Atlantic salmon anglers; unfortunately, the populations of these fish have plummeted, and the Atlantic salmon is now included on the list of federally protected endangered species.

Atlantic salmon fishermen have always put great stock in attractor patterns, flies that imitate nothing in nature but encourage fish to strike out of a sense of anger, curiosity, or territoriality. Many of the most enduring New England streamers are also attractor patterns; if tied on black-japanned hooks that have upturned eyes, they would be right at home in the fly box of an Atlantic salmon fisherman. But the similarities between Atlantic salmon flies and New England streamers run deeper. New England streamers have many of the same components found on Atlantic salmon flies: tinsel tags, hackle-fiber tails and throats, floss bodies, tinsel ribs, feather shoulders, and jungle-cock cheeks.

Other streamers are designed to imitate things fish eat. In the Northeast, smelt are an important forage fish for large landlocked salmon and trout. These baitfish are found in lakes across New England; find a lake producing big salmon and trout, and you're probably fishing water rich in smelt. Most flies designed for trolling are tied to imitate smelt.

Smelt are also important to anglers casting flies into rivers and streams. Smelt congregate at the mouths of rivers in spring soon after ice-out. Within days the smelt begin their annual spawning run into the rushing water. Sometimes the fishing can be fast and furious as large salmon and trout feed on the smelt. Anglers across New England tie streamers throughout the winter, eagerly awaiting the spring smelt run. Smelt have light olive backs and silvery sides, and imitations are tied to duplicate the colors and size of this baitfish. Still, many of these patterns have the same essential components of Atlantic-salmon flies; the difference is the use of materials that duplicate the colors of smelt.

It might be fair to say that New England streamers are the less-complicated cousins of Atlantic salmon flies. One-hundred years ago, Atlantic salmon flies were widely used to catch trout and landlocked salmon. As tiers developed a separate set of streamers for use in the North Woods, the influence of Atlantic salmon flies could be seen in their work. I don't mind a bit: New England streamers are among the most beautiful freshwater patterns ever developed. Though less complicated to tie than a full-dressed Silver Doctor (one of the Atlantic salmon patterns that was commonly used to catch landlocked salmon and trout), they do test the skill of even the most accomplished tiers.

Streamers are also important to fly fishers in other parts of the country. I've always believed in the axiom that big fish eat little fish, and the biggest fish willingly pass up insects in favor of meals of small fish. Streamers are used to catch trout, bass, pike, and all of the other species of gamefish. If you fly fish, you must carry a selection of streamers.

GRAY WOLF'S ORANGE TIGER
designed & tied by Gray Wolf

Tag: Flat silver tinsel.
Body: Light orange floss.
Rib: Flat silver tinsel.
Belly: Peacock herl, white bucktail, and golden pheasant crest feather.
Underwing: Golden pheasant crest feather.
Wings: Yellow, orange, and grizzly hackles.
Shoulders: Golden pheasant breast feathers.
Cheeks: Jungle cock.

The Components of Classic Streamers

Throughout this book I will be referring to various parts of the flies. The nomenclature I use is fairly standardized and understood wherever fly tiers gather. While not all classic streamers contain all of these components, many do. If you're more accustomed to tying simpler trout flies, you'll find tying classic streamers a rewarding challenge.

Let's examine the parts of a streamer as if we were tying a fly, starting at the rear end of the hook shank and working forward.

Tag

The tag is a short piece of material wound on the end of the hook shank. The tag is usually made of tinsel or floss. I prefer to begin the tag on the shank opposite the tip of the barb, and end the tag opposite the tip of the point. Many Atlantic salmon flies have a narrow band of tinsel and then a wider band of floss. This is more common on salmon flies than on classic streamers, but if you examine a fly with this sort of tag, that separate band of tinsel is called the tip.

Tail

Many classic streamers have tails tied at the end of their hook shanks. Hackle fibers are the most commonly used material for making tails, but some fancy patterns have tails of peacock sword fibers and other materials. The length of the tail varies with the pattern and your personal preference. When given a choice, I like a pronounced tail that is usually about one-third the length of the hook shank.

Body

The bodies of classic streamers are usually made of tinsel, floss, chenille, or wool yarn, and cover most of the hook shank. Curiously, very few patterns call for dubbing as a body material.

Rib

The rib is typically made of some sort of tinsel, and is spiral-wrapped up the hook shank on top of the body. The rib gives the body of the fly a segmented appearance and a little fish-attracting flash. Some tiers closely space the ribs on their flies, but I like mine spaced farther apart so I can easily see the material in the body of the fly. Study the photos of the flies in this book and experiment with your own flies to develop your own style of tying.

Belly

What I call the belly of the fly another tier might include in his description of the throat. If I refer to the belly (not all flies have a belly), I'm speaking of the long material—usually bucktail or peacock herl—tied on the bottom of the hook. Typically the length of the belly is equal to the length of the hook shank; on some patterns, the belly extends from the head of the fly past the bend of the hook. The materials in the belly flow back when drawn through the water, helping to give the fly the profile of a baitfish.

Throat

The throat is tied on the bottom of the hook behind the head of the fly. Common materials are hackle and guineafowl fibers, and strips of dyed goose quill. The throat contributes to the profile of the head of a baitfish. A red material is often used to suggest the color of gills.

Underwing

As the name suggests, the underwing is tied under the main wing of the fly. Sometimes the underwing is easy to see, while other times it is almost completely hidden by the wings. Once the fly is wet, however, the color of the underwing may show through and dramatically affect the color of the fly. Bucktail and golden-pheasant crest feathers are commonly used for tying underwings.

Wings

The wings are one of the most outstanding features of classic streamers, especially traditional New England patterns. Most flies are tied with either feather or hair wings; a few streamers, such as the Lady Doctor, have wings made of both hair and feathers.

Silver Pheasant

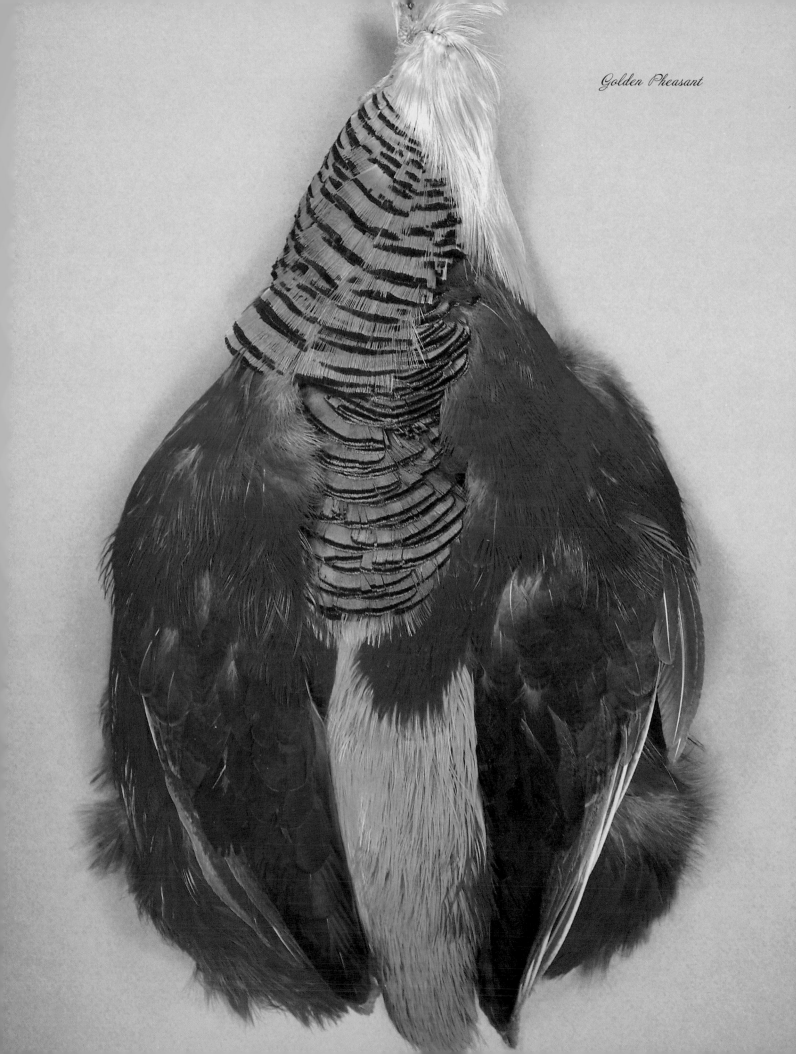

Golden Pheasant

Ring-Necked Pheasant

Lady Amherst Pheasant

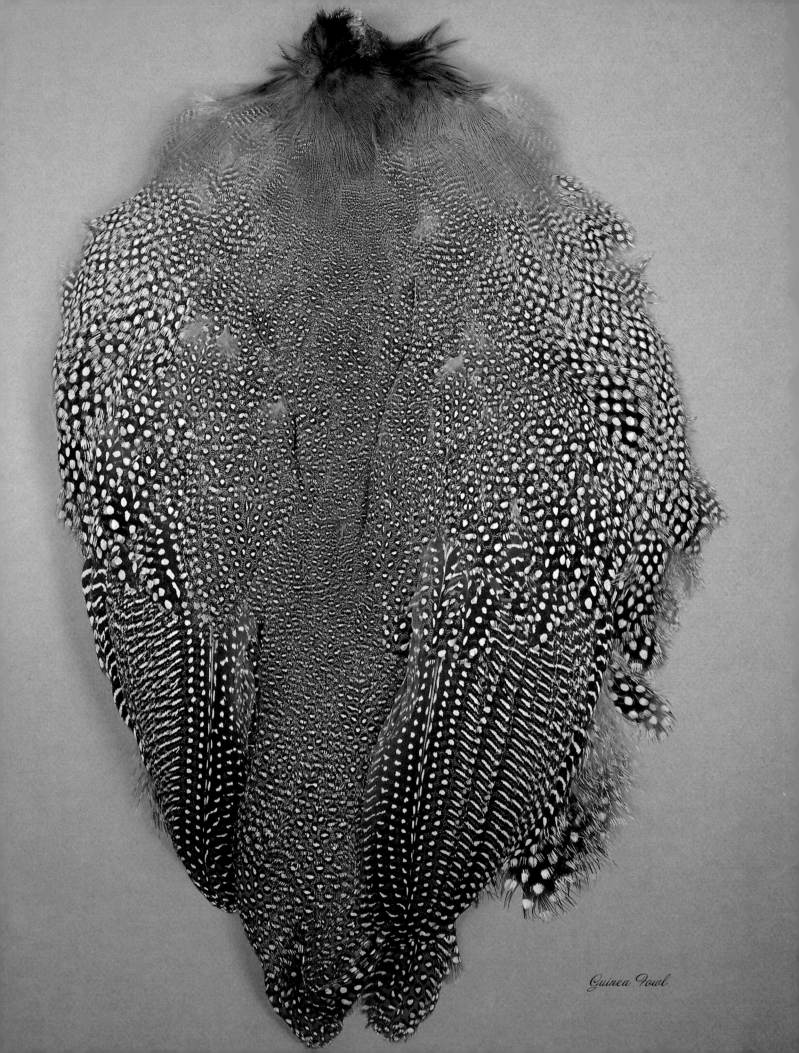

Guinea Fowl

Jungle Cock Cape

There are several types of feather wings. The first are wings made of entire hackles tied on the top or sides of the hook. The feathers give the fly the streamlined torpedo shape of a baitfish.

Wings made of marabou are also popular. It's been said that marabou is one of the most important fly-tying materials, and I agree. Nothing compares to the pulsating, lifelike action of this feather in the water. We will be tying the Ballou Special, a smelt imitation that has a marabou wing.

A few patterns have an entire flank or body feather from a bird tied flat along the top of the hook shank. This feather curls down the sides of the fly and veils the body. When drawn through the water, the feather sweeps back to simulate the thin profile of a baitfish.

There is less variation in the construction of hair wings; the variety comes more with the selection of wing materials. Polar bear, black bear, squirrel tail, and bucktail are all used for tying hair-wing streamers.

Some streamers have "mixed" wings of hair and feathers. An authentic Lady Doctor, for instance, has a wing comprising black-bear hair, polar-bear hair, and two jungle-cock feathers. While mixed wings are very common on classic Atlantic salmon flies, Yankee fly tiers took a more simplified approach and usually relied on either hair or common feathers.

Sometimes the length of the wing for a fly is specified in the recipe, but most of the time it is not. Usually the wing is at least equal to the length of the hook shank, but sometimes it is tied considerably longer. Experiment to see which you prefer; many experienced fishermen, however, dislike flies with wings extending far beyond the hook bend because the material can foul when fishing.

Topping

The topping is tied on top of the wing. Peacock herl is the most commonly used material for tying toppings on classic streamers. Though not a perfect match, the herl is supposed to simulate the olive back of a baitfish.

Shoulders

Shoulders are found almost exclusively on feather-wing streamers. A shoulder is a short feather tied on each side of the wing. They are generally made of some broad body feather, such as that of a silver pheasant or guinea fowl, and are roughly one-third the length of the wing. The shoulders simulate the opaque head of a baitfish, and the feather wing mimics the more transparent tail.

Cheeks

The cheeks are tied on the sides of the shoulders, the sides of the wing, or along the hook shank behind the thread head; it depends upon the pattern and the preference of the tier. The cheeks simulate the eyes of the baitfish, and are usually made of jungle-cock feathers.

Now we have a common nomenclature. I'll refer to these parts of streamers when we tie the flies. Some tiers and authors may describe the parts of a fly slightly differently—such as including the underwing in the recipe for the wing—but these differences are minor.

You'll notice that I occasionally say the dimensions or proportions of parts and materials are left to the discretion of the tier—that's you. I really do mean that. You're tying flies for your own pleasure and use, so feel free to experiment and develop a personal style.

Chapter 2
GETTING THE GOODS FOR TRADITIONAL STREAMERS

*I*t's fairly easy to find quality materials for dressing classic streamers. Some expert tiers moan about how difficult it is to acquire the necessary ingredients, probably to discourage newcomers and limit the number of members to their club. The truth is that almost any well-stocked fly shop has everything you need to tie nice streamers. As you gain skill at tying these flies, you'll develop an eye for distinguishing between prime ingredients for dressing presentation-quality streamers, and good materials for tying flies for fishing. A novice should first concentrate on tying "fish" flies, and have fun.

Of course, it's not enough to just buy a box of hooks and package of feathers. There are a few things you should know when selecting ingredients. Let's examine the different materials you'll need to tie classic streamers and learn some of the finer points of choosing quality ingredients.

HOOKS

It's said that the hook is the chassis on which a fly is built. I would add one other thing: The hook is also the first link between you and the fish.

There are a lot of excellent hooks available for tying streamers. Rather than getting into a laundry list of company names and model numbers, which will change over time, let me share some general descriptions of streamer hooks and their specific applications.

The length of the shank is the most outstanding feature of a streamer hook. Most streamer hooks have what are called 4X-, 6X-, or 8X-long shanks, but I've also seen some oddball designations of 5X and 7X long. There are also a couple of manufacturers offering 10X-long hooks which they attribute to famed Maine streamer tier Carrie Stevens—we'll be tying her famous Gray Ghost—but it's doubtful she tied many flies on such gargantuan irons. Most of the streamers we are learning to tie were originally dressed on 4X- to 8X-long hooks.

There is no industry-wide standard for hook-shank length designation. One company's 8X-long hook, for example, might be a little shorter or longer than another manufacturer's hook. This is important to know when following a recipe for a fly from a book or magazine; the fly you tie could look slightly different from the one in the illustration because the author might have used another brand of hooks. Don't let this bother you; any difference will be very minor.

When selecting long-shank hooks for tying streamers for fishing, my advice is to concentrate on the overall length of the finished fly rather than the manufacturer's designation of hook-shank length. Let's continue using 8X-long hooks as our example. Suppose the minnows in your favorite trout stream are 2 inches long. You have a proven pattern for a streamer that imitates a minnow calling for an 8X-long hook. The fly you tie might have a tail, and the hair or feathers in the wing and belly might hang out past the bend of the hook. To tie this fly so that it imitates those minnows, you'll need to use a hook with a shank that is 1½ to 1¾ inches long. This translates into about a size 8, 8X-long hook. If

you're a stickler for accuracy, you'll put one of those hooks in the vise and start tying. What I would do, however, is another thing.

I'm not a fan of 8X-long hooks that are smaller than size 6. Why should I use hooks with narrow gaps if I don't have to? Rather than worrying about the numeric designation of hook-shank length, I would concentrate on the length of those minnows and choose size 4, 6X-long hooks. With these I can tie flies of the proper length and have hooks with larger gaps, thus increasing my chances at catching fish.

The eye is a very important component of a streamer hook. An improperly designed hook eye will give you fits when trying to complete the head of a fly. There are also times when a correctly made eye can help you tie a streamer. How the eye will help me tie the streamer is one of the criteria I use for selecting a hook.

Contemporary hooks come with either looped eyes or ring eyes. Bending back, or looping, the end of the

hook shank forms the looped eye. This type of eye is very traditional and still used on Atlantic salmon and some freshwater streamer hooks. Looped-eye hooks were used by many of the tiers who originated the patterns we are studying.

If you want to tie completely authentic streamers with hooks that have looped eyes, try to use only hooks that are described as having "tapered-loop" eyes. This term means that the end of the wire is tapered to a point before it is bent back to form the eye. A tapered-loop eye allows you to make a neat transition as you wrap thread and materials from the hook shank up to the eye. Some manufacturers do not taper the wire before creating the loop, and you'll be left to figure out how to get the thread and body materials from the shank up to the eye; it's tough to make a smooth transition using this type of hook.

A looped eye can actually help you tie flies with wings mounted on top of the hook. The doubled wire where the loop is formed creates a small platform on which to set the wings. On the other hand, if you want to tie a fly with the wings mounted on the sides of the hook, such as the famous Gray Ghost feather-wing streamer, the wire that is looped back can get in the way of positioning the feathers.

The ring eye is the second type of hook eye. Today this is the most widely used type of eye on fly hooks. The ring eye will not interfere as you tie the body of the fly. It also won't be in the way if you dress a streamer with feather wings mounted on the sides of the fly. On the other hand, you'll miss the advantage of having that little platform when tying flies with top-mounted wings. Both types of eyes are acceptable; each simply has its advantages and disadvantages that you should weigh when selecting hooks.

The bend, point, and barb are at the other end of the hook. You'll obviously want to select hooks that have the sharpest possible points. Some industrious tiers sharpen every hook before it goes into the fly-tying vise, but I'm lazy and would quickly lose the sharpening stone. I'm relieved that most hooks come with very sharp points. With respect to barbs, the trend toward catch-and-release fishing has encouraged some manufacturers to make premium hooks that have small barbs. These barbs are designed to aid anglers in releasing fish; some say that these small barbs also aid hook penetration and help us catch more fish. Maybe this is true.

There are many different styles of hook bends. Most vintage streamer hooks had either Limerick or Sproat bends, and hooks with these bends are still widely available. Some manufacturers, however, make streamer hooks with round bends. I don't believe there is an advantage in using one style of bend over another; they seem to hook fish equally well.

Despite what the manufacturers claim, I am sad to say that very few companies are making what I would call a true "classic" streamer hook. Several manufacturers offer hooks that they say are for tying traditional streamers, and one comes very close to meeting all of our requirements: their hook is 7X-long, made of heavy wire, and has a Limerick bend and tapered-loop eye. For some reason, though, the eye is made straight out from the hook shank rather than bent down. Virtually all of the classic patterns I have examined—those actually tied by Carrie Stevens, Bill Edson, Herbert Welch and the other famous streamer fly tiers—were tied on hooks having turned-down eyes. And check out the flies illustrated in the authoritative books of Col. Joseph Bates; almost all are tied on hooks with bent-down eyes. If this company would take the extra step of bending down the eyes on those hooks, it would have a true classic freshwater streamer hook. This hook is excellent, however, for tying the Thunder Creek series of flies. I consider those patterns as modern classics, and they should definitely have a place in your fly box.

For dressing really authentic-looking classic streamers, I suggest using the wonderful hooks offered by Gaelic Supreme and Castle Arms. Both of these companies are importing into the United States lovely English-made hooks for tying your finest streamers. Gaelic Supreme, which is run by Grahame Maisey, sells the Mike Martinek Rangeley Streamer hooks. Mike Martinek is one of the leaders at tying classic New England streamers. Grahame and Mike teamed together to develop a series of hooks based on the traditional Allcock hooks used during the first half of the 20th century. At the time of this writing, they are offering these hooks in a variety of sizes with 6X- and 8X- long shanks, but they plan to introduce a 10X-long hook for dressing presentation flies.

Castle Arms, which is owned by Phil Castleman, offers the Allcock Streamer Hook. These 8X-long hooks are first rate and suited for creating really show-quality streamers. Phil is also a leader is selling rare and unusual fly-tying materials. (You'll find the contact information for both Gaelic Supreme and Castle Arms in the appendix of this book.)

In addition tying streamers on single-shank hooks, you can also dress flies on tandem-hook rigs. These flies are used for trolling early in the season after ice-out. A lot of fly fishermen look down their noses at trolling; I used to be one of them. Then, a number of years ago, I was fishing New Brunswick's Miramichi River for spring Atlantic salmon. These fish had entered the river the previous summer and fall, and spent the winter in the frigid water under the ice. They were now dropping back out to sea, and I spent most of the week wading the cold water, watching chunks of ice flow by. Then, near the end of the week, a Canadian friend suggested we spend a morning trolling the big part of the river near Red Bank. Though it sleeted and rained all day, I felt warm and comfortable. It was great being in a boat and out of that icy river.

Tandem hooks are designed to give anglers an advantage on hooking fish that "strike short," but I don't know if a big fish really attacks the tail of a smaller baitfish: Most anglers agree that fish key in on the eyes of prey. Nevertheless, many fish are hooked every season on trailing "stinger" hooks. I use 2X-long wet fly hooks to make tandem-hook rigs. Where regulations permit, treble hooks are sometimes used for stingers.

I can't give you a firm recommendation on which hooks to use. I do like those Gaelic Supreme and Castle Arms hooks, but you'll have to order those from the distributors. If your goal is to tie authentic-looking classic streamers, take the time to order those hooks. The flies in this book are tied on several different brands and styles of hooks. When selecting hooks to tie flies for fishing, I usually concern myself with the overall length of the finished flies, and then think about how the hook eyes can help me tie on the wings.

THREAD

I started tying flies when I was about twelve years old. I had a spool of black thread that came with a beginner's fly-tying kit, and didn't know it was anything special from other thin threads. I raided my mother's sewing basket when I decided to add more colors of thread to my collection of fly-tying materials. Okay, so I'm not the only guy to have ever swiped a spool or two from his mother's or wife's sewing basket—what's the big deal? Well, I took it a step further.

I owned only one fly-tying book, and I spent hours pouring over it. In the chapter on materials, the author mentioned "prewaxed" thread. I had never heard of that before. What could it be? I scratched my head for a while, and came up with the perfect solution for creating what I believed would be a marvelous fly-tying thread.

I gathered up those spools of sewing thread and headed to the kitchen. I got out a pot and found a box of canning wax. I melted the wax in the pot, dropped in the thread, and made my own waxed thread. And that's just what I had: spools of thread with caked wax.

Thread is probably the most overlooked material in fly tying. Tiers go to great lengths to select quality hooks, feathers, and other ingredients, and then give little thought to the thing that holds their flies together: the thread. There are many exceptional threads on the market, and some are surprisingly strong for their narrow sizes. Many years ago, tiers used silk thread. This was beautiful material, but it had the tendency to fray when used and even decompose over time. If you look hard, you will still be able to find real silk thread, but I don't know why you'd want to use it; modern tying threads offer so many more advantages. Today, every fly shop and fly-tying catalog stocks nylon and polyester threads; most of the flies in this book are tied with these types of threads.

You'll need a spool of stout white thread, preferably size 6/0. Use this for tying bodies that are made with light-colored materials, especially red, orange and yellow flosses. When the fly gets wet, the floss becomes slightly transparent and a dark-colored thread bleeds through the body and spoils the appearance of the fly. After you have tied the body and are ready to add the wings, secure the white thread with a whip finish, clip, and switch to the color of thread you'll use to tie the head of the fly.

Black size 8/0 or 6/0 thread is used for tying the bodies of flies that are made of black floss or entirely of tinsel or chenille. The black thread doesn't bleed through these body materials when the fly gets wet, and it is convenient to use the same spool of thread for tying the entire fly.

You'll want separate spools of thread for tying the heads on your flies. A small head is one of the qualities of a superior New England feather-wing streamer. Even flies with bucktail wings can have remarkably small heads if you plan ahead. Use the correct ingredients, and make every wrap count. It's easier to tie a small head using size 8/0 thread. You'll need a spool of black, plus any other colors you may want to use. When I tie the body with white size 6/0 thread, I always switch to the narrower diameter thread to complete the streamer. I must confess, however, that when I dress a body with black thread, I usually use size 6/0 thread throughout.

Finally, every fly-tying kit should include a spool of Kevlar thread. Kevlar comes in a limited number of colors and is virtually unbreakable; if you secure a spool of Kevlar to a heavy-wire hook and begin pulling on the thread, the Kevlar will probably cut into your fingers before it snaps. I use Kevlar for constructing tandem-hook rigs. I also use a separate set of scissors for cutting Kevlar (as well as tinsel and wire) rather than the scissors I use for cutting flosses, threads, hairs, and other soft materials. Tough Kevlar can ruin a pair of fine blades.

You may substitute Monocord, size 3/0 thread, or one of the new gel-spun threads for the Kevlar. These threads are very strong, and you can use a lot of tension when wrapping them on the hook. While Kevlar is my first choice for attaching wire to the tandem hooks of a trolling fly, size 3/0 thread and Monocord come in a greater range of colors. All of these stout threads are also excellent for spinning deer hair for tying Muddler Minnows.

FLOSSES, TINSELS, & OTHER BODY MATERIALS

Floss is used for tying the bodies of many streamers. The early fly tiers used beautiful silk flosses. Silk floss is still available, and it's my first choice when tying really authentic reproductions of classic streamers. Today, however, there are many excellent substitutes made of Rayon, polyester, nylon, and Dacron. These flosses are extremely strong and come in many superb colors.

Some standard, nonstretch flosses are packaged one strand per spool, while others have four strands per spool. There is no real advantage to using one type of spool over another. Some tiers place a spool of single-strand floss in a bobbin and use it like thread, while others cut off pieces of floss from one of the strands of a four-strand spool. The advantage to using a spool of single-strand floss in a bobbin is that it stays cleaner because you avoid rubbing your fingers up and down the material as you wrap the floss on the hook. Of course, anyone who doesn't wash the grime and oils from his hands before he ties flies (or wraps

the guides on a fishing rod) gets what he deserves.

Stretch-nylon floss is also an excellent product. Stretch nylon lies flat when wrapped on the hook shank, is durable, and maintains its color when wet. It comes in a variety of shades, including fluorescent colors. This single-strand material is perfect for using with a bobbin. If you do try to use your floss in a bobbin, be aware that the individual strands twist together as you wrap the material on the hook, preventing you from tying a smooth body. To remedy this, let the spool hang and unwind after every dozen wraps.

Chenille is also used to tie the bodies on classic streamers. Traditional chenille is a fuzzy material, usually short cotton fibers spun between strands of thread. Chenille is durable, easy to use, and comes in a wide variety of colors and sizes. Avoid buying wide chenille because it makes very bulky bodies. For our purposes, narrow- and medium-width chenille is the most useful.

Angora wool yarn is a valuable material for tying the bodies of streamers. I think it is listed in many older patterns because a fly tier could always find it in the family sewing basket; today we have more interesting materials and have largely discarded yarn. This is unfortunate because it is widely available and comes in so many colors.

The bodies of most streamers have a bit of tinsel. Whether making a small tag at the end of the hook shank, wrapping a rib, or tying the entire body, tinsel gives a streamer fish-attracting flash. Real metal tinsel is frustrating stuff that easily breaks and tarnishes. I recommend Mylar tinsel. Mylar tinsel comes in several sizes, is silver on one side and gold on the other, and will not tarnish.

I read in a book written by one leading fly-tying authority that Mylar tinsel isn't very strong, but I disagree. I'm surprised just how hard I can horse Mylar; I use really firm tension when wrapping Mylar tinsel to get it to lie flat and smooth, and I am very pleased with the results.

Some fly recipes call for embossed tinsel. Embossed Mylar tinsel is available, but it is softer than metal tinsel and doesn't really maintain the embossing when wrapped on the hook. Metal embossed tinsel, however, can break and tarnish. Why put up with the frustration?

Here's where I cheat; unless I'm tying a presentation fly, I substitute flat Mylar for the embossed tinsel.

Oval tinsel is used on many streamers and comes in three diameters: narrow, medium, and wide. It is most commonly used as ribbing over floss and flat-tinsel bodies. You'll occasionally find patterns calling for silver or gold twist, which is a type of tinsel thread. Twist is difficult to find, but round tinsel is a good substitute. If you insist on using twist, inquire at shops catering to Atlantic-salmon fly tiers; these guys still use twist, as well as all sorts of bizarre materials.

FEATHERS

Now we're jumping into the deep end of the lake. Quality feathers are very important for tying nice streamers, especially the classic New England streamers. They're also one of the least understood materials.

Let's start with the hackles used for tying wings. Good hackles have full, rounded ends; skinny hackles create flies that look more like swimming pencils than baitfish. Ideal hackles have strong, stiff center barbs to help prevent the feathers from wrapping around the hook when you cast and fish the fly. Most saltwater patterns are tied with flimsy hackle to give those flies pulsating action, but these feathers make poor freshwater streamers.

I prefer choosing feathers for wings from either hackle capes or packages of strung hackle. I have several hackle capes described by the producer as "streamer necks." All of these are full of good, usable feathers. These capes are inexpensive (the big money for hackle producers is in high-quality dry-fly hackle) and come in a wide range of colors.

If you can spend a few extra dollars, check out the American Rooster line of capes offered by Whiting Farms. Dr. Tom Whiting is the modern guru of growing fly-tying feathers. The hackles on his American Rooster line are the perfect shape for tying the wings on streamers. These capes come in a full range of natural and dyed colors, so you'll be able to tie the wings on almost any classic pattern, and invent dozens of original streamers. And a new company, flytyervariant.com, offers a complete set of Whiting Farms's coq de Leon

capes created specifically for tying streamer wings. This set includes over twenty capes in a variety of natural and dyed colors. You can also select individual capes if you're not interested in purchasing an entire set.

Finally, almost every fly shop stocks packages of strung hackle. There will be some waste when working with strung hackle, as you'll see when we make the wings for the Gray Ghost, but any feathers that don't make the grade for tying streamers can be used for dressing other patterns. I prefer using domestic rather than Chinese hackle because the domestic feathers usually have thinner center quills that allow me to tie flies with small heads.

I should say a word about hackle and color selection. As I pointed out when we covered hooks and flosses, many of the materials used by fly tiers sixty years ago are no longer available. This is particularly true with dyed hackle. Many of the dyes used at that time are no longer available, and consequently it is difficult to duplicate the colors found on vintage flies. Also, the original colors on an old fly may have faded over the years, making it impossible to know what the streamer looked like when it was new and sitting in the vise. Some fastidious tiers spend years experimenting with dyes in order to replicate the original colors, and I admire their determination. Don't despair if you can't find hackles in the exact shades used half a century ago; select quality feathers in colors that most approximate the original hues.

Many feather-wing streamers also have shorter feathers on the front one-third of the wings. This part of the fly is called the shoulder. These feathers imitate the opaque head of the baitfish. Teal and mallard flank, guinea-fowl, and silver-pheasant body feathers, and many of the body feathers from ring-necked, Reeves, and golden pheasants are all useful for making shoulders. These feathers can be used in their natural colors, or may be dyed to tie some original and beautiful flies.

To imitate the eyes of the baitfish, a jungle-cock neck feather, sometimes called a "nail," is placed on each shoulder or on the sides of the wing. Real jungle cock is an expensive but necessary ingredient for tying authentic classic patterns. If you're not a stickler for accuracy, imitation jungle cock is widely available, but it is not

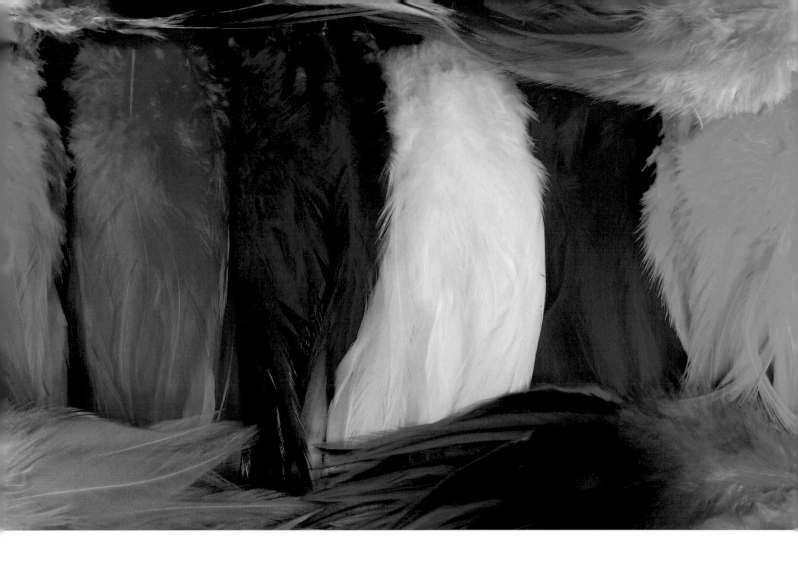

your best choice. Rather than use the fake nails, you can omit the jungle cock from your flies and still tie attractive, fish-catching streamers.

Many other feathers are used to tie streamers. Marabou, one of the most lifelike materials when drawn through the water, is used as wings and throats. Golden-pheasant crests are used as tails, underwings, and even on the bellies of streamers. Strips of dyed goose or turkey are used as throats, wings, and tails. Peacock herl and sword fibers are used to wrap bodies and make tails, bellies and wings. Hackle fibers and guinea-fowl feathers are used to tie tails and throats.

Just about any feather can be used to tie streamers. You're limited only by your imagination.

HAIRS & FURS

You'll occasionally find recipes for classic streamers recommending some rare hair or fur. Except for a few materials, such as polar-bear hair, the early tiers used materials that came from the North Woods. Chief among these ingredients is bucktail.

The term "bucktail" is somewhat of a misnomer. With many states allowing the hunting of at least a limited number of does, who's to say whether a deer tail came from a buck or a doe? Of course, it's not important to know the gender of the deer providing the tail; I just wanted to point out this little curiosity of the fly-tying vocabulary.

When purchasing a bucktail, don't just grab the biggest tail off the fly-shop rack; it may not be the best for tying streamers. Fly-tying material wholesalers get goods from all over the United States. As a result, they have deer tails (and body hair) from many subspecies of deer. The northern woodland whitetail and the Dakota whitetail are the largest North American whitetail deer, and the tails from these animals can be very large (up to 14 inches from the base of the tail to the tips of the end hairs). Unfortunately, the hairs on these tails are usually thick and course. By comparison, many southeastern deer are smaller and the hairs on their tails have a finer, less course texture. While it may seem that you're getting more material with the bigger tails, you'll tie nicer streamers using smaller tails that have finer hairs.

Select bucktails that have the straightest hair; this hair makes neater, sleeker flies. Also look for tails with the fewest number of broken hairs. You'll need a collection of bucktails. Natural white bucktail is used for the wings and bellies on many streamers, but so is bucktail dyed red, orange, and yellow.

Red and gray squirrel tails are also useful; you'll find patterns with wings made from natural and dyed squirrel-tail hair.

Several classic patterns call for black-bear and polar-bear hair. Patches of black-bear hair are widely available. Unfortunately, much of this is body hair, which is very course and twisted. I recently tossed out a bag full of black-bear hair; while the material was in excellent condition, the hair really wasn't good for anything. Look through the packages of black-bear hair at your local fly shop and select the patch with the straightest hairs. If you ever have an opportunity to acquire the mask—or face—of a black bear, grab it; this hair is straight and perfect for fly tying.

Polar-bear hair has a natural translucency that gives the wings of flies a wonderful ethereal look. I remember examining some polar-bear hair during a visit to the Philadelphia Museum of Natural History. After entering the doors of the museum, you ascend a flight of stairs that was guarded by two stuffed polar bears. (Today those bears have been moved to another part of the museum.) I stopped at the top of the stairs near one of the bears, bent over, and observed the light passing through the hairs. The bright, translucent quality of the hair was amazing. Gosh, I thought, if I only had a pair of scissors (just kidding). After a moment, I stood and turned to go— and noticed two security guards standing behind me. Maybe they thought I really did have a pair of scissors.

Polar-bear hair is one of those natural materials that hasn't been duplicated. It is legal to possess and use polar bear, and I know of one dealer who purchases polar-bear hides (usually old rugs), cuts them into small patches, and packages the material for fly tiers. While the quality of the material is excellent, it is expensive. Use it if you can afford it, and God bless you.

For the rest of us, white or cream sheep's hair is one of the best substitutes I know for polar bear. It comes in a variety of lengths, but even the shorter hairs—about 2 inches long—are excellent for tying streamers. Bleached raccoon tail hair is also a good substitute for polar-bear hair. Though not my first choice, white bucktail is a common substitute for polar bear. And finally, if you're not a fanatic with respect to materials selection, there are some nice synthetic hairs on the market that do an admirable job at imitating polar-bear hair (although I don't think this was the intent of the manufacturers). The biggest drawback with synthetic hair is that it lacks the natural taper of real hair, and is a very poor choice for tying framed flies; however, if your goal is to tie "fishing" flies, synthetic hair is an excellent and inexpensive choice.

So, where do you begin collecting materials for dressing streamers? Start by concentrating on only a few flies. Select patterns that complement one another and have interchangeable materials. Don't look at the flies we're going to tie as static patterns that can't be changed; view them as "forms" (that's how I've chosen them) and feel free to substitute with different colored materials. And please don't buy into the dogma that you must have rare—and in some cases antique— materials to tie classic streamers. The guys who talk this way are usually sitting on the largest collections of these materials and want the rest of use to think that we're not worthy to enjoy these wonderful flies. Use readily available materials that make nice streamers— and have fun!

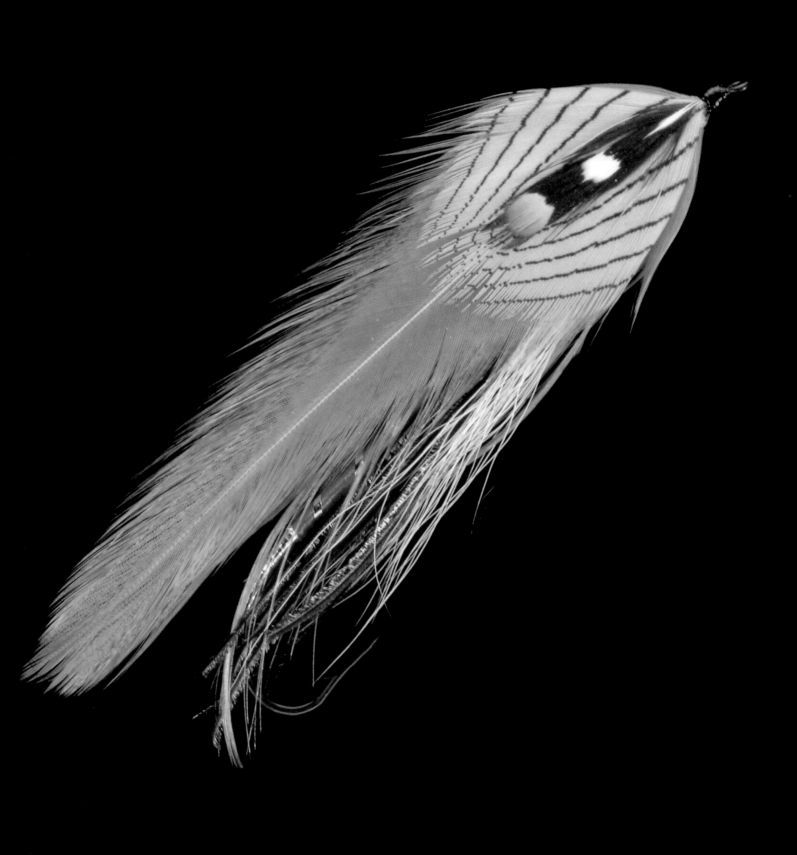

Chapter 3
DRESSING THE CLASSIC GRAY GHOST

The Gray Ghost is the most famous of the classic New England streamers. It was designed in the 1930s by Mrs. Carrie Stevens, of Upper Dam and Madison, Maine. A hatmaker by trade, Carrie Stevens designed dozens of beautiful streamers. The story of she and her husband is legendary; she tied the flies, and her husband, Wallace, took the clients fishing. Mrs. Stevens designed the Gray Ghost to imitate a smelt, and on her first outing with the new fly she caught a 6-pound, 13-ounce brook trout with which she won second prize in the annual *Field & Stream* magazine fishing derby.

The outstanding feature of the Gray Ghost is the feather wings positioned on the sides of the hook shank. Most Northeast fly fishers recognize this as the Stevens—or Rangeley—style of tying. This design helps give the fly the streamlined look of a smelt or other baitfish. Hundreds of patterns, dressed with the wings on the sides of the hooks, have been developed. In homage to Stevens, many of these flies have the word "Ghost" somewhere in their names.

Let's use the Gray Ghost as our example for tying a streamer with feather wings mounted on the sides of the fly. Everything I am using to tie Gray Ghost can be found in just about any fly shop, but I should say something about hook selection. Most Gray Ghosts that I have examined, including those tied by Mrs. Stevens, were dressed on hooks having extra-long shanks. A couple of manufacturers are offering 10X-long hooks they describe as their "Carrie Stevens" models, but I've never seen one of her

flies tied on such huge hooks (although she may very well have used such hooks). Even Col. Bates, who probably owned the largest collection of original Stevens flies, wrote that she usually used 5X-long hooks. Today, most tiers use 6X- to 8X-long hooks for dressing the Gray Ghost, and these make really attractive streamers. Since the wings are tied on the sides of the fly, choose a hook with a ring eye; this type of eye won't interfere when you tie on the feather wings. Here's what you'll need to tie Gray Ghost:

Hook: 8X-long streamer hook, sizes 6 to 2.
Thread: White, size 6/0 for tying the body, and black, size 8/0 for tying the head.
Tag: Flat silver tinsel.
Body: Orange floss.
Rib: Flat silver tinsel.
Belly: Peacock herl, white bucktail, and a golden-pheasant crest feather.
Throat: Gray hackle fibers.
Underwing: Golden-pheasant crest.
Wings: Gray saddle hackles.
Shoulders: Silver-pheasant body feathers.
Cheeks: Jungle cock.

CRAFTING THE WINGS

I'll bet more people read this book to learn how to make the feather wings for the Gray Ghost than for any other reason. It's challenging—this isn't the starting point when learning to tie flies—but any moderately accomplished tier can learn to craft the wings and dress the fly.

Mrs. Stevens glued together the feathers that made the individual wings of her streamers; some say she got the idea from her experience as a hatmaker. Her method makes the flies durable, and the wings are easier to tie to the hook. After preparing all of the wings, she would then assemble the flies. If you can spare only an hour or so in the evenings for your fly tying, make the wings for several streamers in one sitting; come back later to complete the flies. This method is quicker, and you'll keep your fly-tying area less cluttered.

The wings on a Gray Ghost and almost all other New England feather-wing streamers have right- and left-hand sides. The Gray Ghost requires two gray hackles for each wing. These hackles can come from either a cape or package of strung hackle. Selecting the feathers from a cape is simple. Hold the neck upright in front of you (with the ends of the hackles pointing down). Select two hackles from the right and two hackles from the left side of the skin. The hackles taken from the right side are used to make the right wing of the streamer; the feathers taken from the left side are used to tie the left wing.

The procedure for choosing feathers from a package of strung hackle is a little more complicated. Start by taking a dozen hackles from the package. Put back into the package any feathers that have thin, skinny ends; these can be used for tying other flies, but not a Gray Ghost. Also reject any feathers that are bent, curved, or otherwise deformed, as well as any that are overly webbed.

Next, examine the strength of the quills of the remaining feathers. An ideal streamer hackle is not so stiff that it lacks action when drawn through the water, but is strong enough so that it doesn't droop too much when held horizontal. Hackles with strong quills are less likely to foul around the hook when fishing. Take each feather, one at a time, and hold it parallel to your tying table. If the feather seems flimsy and droops, flip it over to see if it stands out straighter on the other side. Feathers that are uniformly weak go back into the package; those that show the ability to stand out fairly straight when tied to a hook remain on the table.

Divide the feathers into two groups for tying the right and left wings of the fly. Take one of the hackles in your right hand and hold it horizontal with the tip pointing to the left. If the feather stands out fairly straight, it will be used for making the right-side wing (if you're a right-handed tier, that will be on the side of the fly facing you); if it droops, flip it over to double-check its strength for being used for the left wing. Divide all of the feathers into right- and left-wing piles.

The Gray Ghost has shoulders made of silver-pheasant body feathers. If you pick feathers from a silver-pheasant skin, select a feather from the right side and one from the left side of the skin. A feather from the right side of the skin is used for making the right shoulder of a streamer; a feather from the left side is used for constructing the left shoulder.

If you use packaged silver-pheasant feathers, you can quickly match together right- and left-side shoulders. Remove the feathers from the package. Select several feathers that have approximately the same number and width of black bars; this will give the shoulders a uniform look. Hold a feather horizontal in front of you with the tip pointing to the left. If the quill of the feather curves up slightly, use it to tie the right wing; if it curves down, use it to tie the left wing (it will curve up when flipped over and tied to the other side of the fly). Divide the silver-pheasant feathers into right- and left-side piles.

If you want to tie a really authentic Gray Ghost, you must include jungle-cock cheeks. I like a pronounced jungle-cock eye, and the "nails" I use are equal to two-thirds the length of the silver-pheasant shoulder—maybe a little longer. Jungle cock is normally straight, so you don't have to worry about dividing the feathers into right- and left-side groups.

Each complete wing of a Gray Ghost is made of two hackles, one silver-pheasant feather, and one jungle-cock nail feather. We'll construct the wings first, and then tie the fly.

1. Selecting the proper hackle is the first step in making nice wings. One option is to pluck feathers from necks such as Whiting American grade capes. Another popular method is to sort through bunches of strung hackle. Let's start with the feathers that will not make proper feather wings. These two hackles have entirely too much web. These feathers will make poor wings, but the fibers are excellent for fashioning into the throats of classic streamers.

2. This hackle has a nice even curvature. It might make one half of a wing. The first step is to test the strength of its quill. Hold the hackle parallel to the top of your tying bench. This hackle droops too much and will foul around the hook when fished. Proceed to the next step to see if it might still work for creating the wing of a streamer.

3. Flip the hackle over to see if it will stand out straighter on the other side. This feather has a "strong" side, and can be used to make the left-side wing. Divide your feathers into two piles: those for making right-side and left-side wings.

4. Select a hackle to form the inside of the wing. Apply a drop of thick cement along the base of the quill. (I use old head cement for this task.)

5. Align and press a second hackle on top of the first feather. Note the nice, rounded ends of this wing.

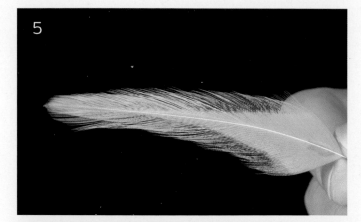

6. Strip the fibers from the base of a silver pheasant body feather. The shoulder should equal about one-third the length of the wing. Apply a drop of think cement along the quill of the hackle, and press the silver pheasant feather into place.

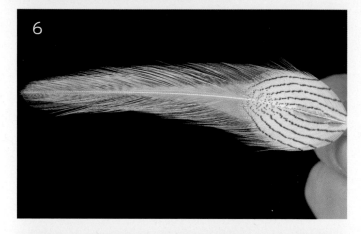

7. Strip the fibers from the base of a jungle cock feather. Apply a drop of cement on the back of the feather.

8. Press the jungle cock feather on top of the silver pheasant shoulder. Here we see one completed Gray Ghost wing. Select the feathers for the matching wing. Construct that wing, and proceed with tying the fly.

TYING THE GRAY GHOST

The wings are made, and we've collected the rest of the materials for tying the Gray Ghost. If you're a moderately accomplished tier, you should have no trouble tying this classic streamer. The body, belly, and underwing are easy, but placing the wings is a bit more challenging. Work slowly until you learn the procedure, and don't despair if things don't work the first time: just unwrap the thread, remove the wings, and try again.

The best advice I can give you is to plan ahead, and make every wrap of thread count. Bulldogging forward and not leaving ample room on the hook for the next materials, and making lots of superfluous thread wraps, will lead to disappointment. Be thoughtful, and you'll tie a nice streamer.

Let's tie the classic Gray Ghost!

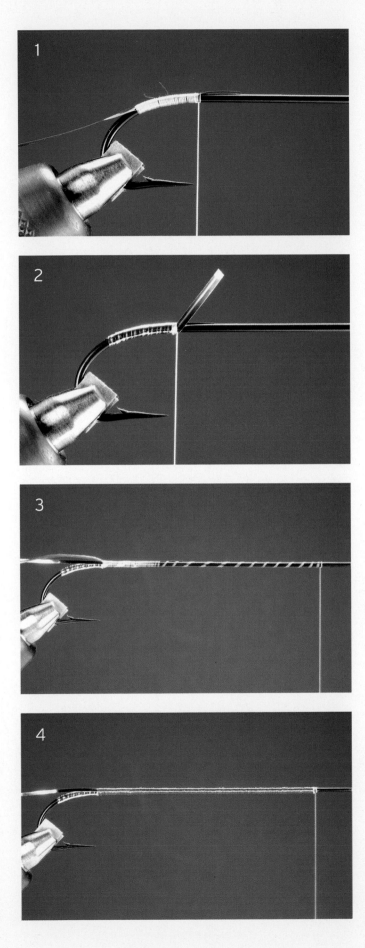

1. Start the white thread near the end of the hook shank. To make a flat base for the tinsel tag, I start the thread on the shank opposite the hook point. Place the tinsel on top of the hook, and wrap the thread down and back up the shank.

2. Wrap the tinsel up the shank to form the tag, tie off, and clip most of the excess; leave a small amount of excess tinsel to wrap under the body. The small amount of extra tinsel helps to create a smooth transition from the tag to the body.

 The length of the tag is a matter of personal preference. I like a slightly longer tag. The tag on this fly begins opposite the tip of the hook barb, and ends opposite the hook point; that's the way I tie the tags on most of my streamers. The idea is to tie the parts on your flies using similar proportions; that's one of the attributes of a well-tied collection of flies.

3. Tie on a piece of narrow tinsel, and then a piece of orange floss. To keep the bulk down, tie the tinsel down using three or four firm wraps of thread. Next, unwind all but the first wrap of thread. Place the orange floss on top of the hook, and make three of four firm wraps of thread. Don't make the wraps on top of one another, but work up the hook shank. Spiral-wrap the thread up the shank to the point where the body will end.

4. Wrap the floss about three-quarters of the way up the hook shank to form the body of the fly. A rotating vise is a great aid for tying a smooth floss body. If you don't have a rotating vise, pass the floss from hand to hand while you work; don't allow the floss to twist tight or it will create a body with lots of little ridges. If you do use only one hand to wrap the body, the floss will twist and tighten while you work; be sure to occasionally spin the bobbin of floss in a counterclockwise direction to remove the twist and keep the floss going on flat and smooth.

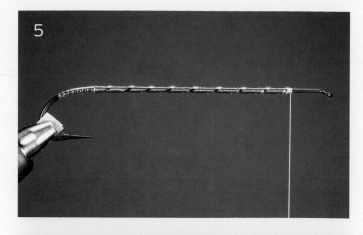

5. Spiral-wrap the tinsel rib up the body. Here again, how you space the tinsel wraps is a personal preference; I space the wraps fairly wide apart so most of the orange body shows through.

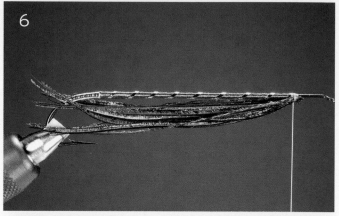

6. Now it's time to make the belly of the fly. Tie several strands of peacock herl under the hook. The herl should extend from the front of the body to past the hook bend. Three firm wraps of thread are all that's needed to secure the herl to the hook.

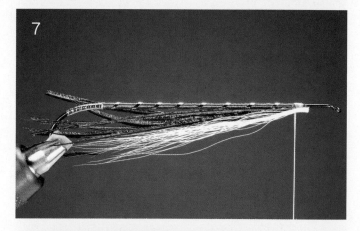

7. Clip a narrow bunch of white bucktail. Straight hair, like that shown on the fly in the photo, makes a neat, trim fly. Unwind all but the first wrap holding the peacock herl, place the bucktail under the fly, and make four firm wraps; these wraps of thread will secure both the herl and bucktail.

8. Let's tie on the underwing and the bottom of the belly. These parts are made of golden-pheasant crest feathers. These feathers come from the top of the head of the male golden pheasant. Most crest feathers are bent and will not lie neatly on the fly. We can fix the feather shown in the photo using the simple procedure described in the next step.

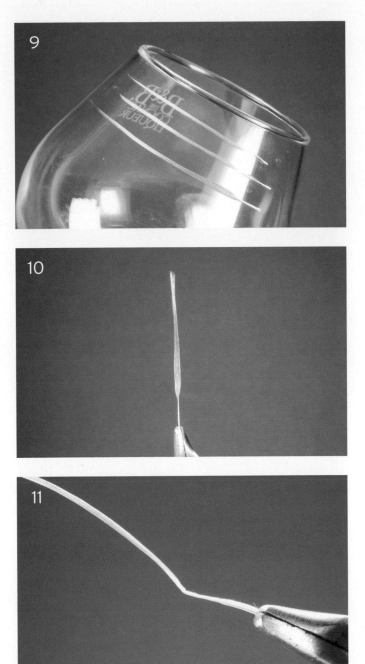

9. Soak the crest feathers in water for an hour. Place the softened feathers on a small glass; a whiskey shot glass or a brandy snifter is about right. A tapered glass, like the brandy snifter shown in the photograph, will allow you to make straight crest feathers with different curvatures. Make sure the feathers are straight and the barbules are close together. Allow the crests to dry before removing them from the glass.

10. Here's the same crest feather we saw in step eight. I soaked this feather in water, and shaped it on a brandy snifter. The stem is straight, and the feather can be used to tie a neat fly.

11. Select a long, straight crest feather for the underwing. This feather should extend from the front of the body to past the hook bend. Flatten and bend the base of the stem using needle-nose pliers or a hemostat.
Select a shorter crest for the bottom of the belly; this feather should extend from the front of the floss body to about half the length of the bucktail belly. Flatten and bend the base of this stem using needle-nose pliers or a hemostat.

12. Tie the long crest feather to the top of the fly. The underwing should curve down over the hook bend.

13. Tie the shorter crest feather on the bottom of the fly, curving up.

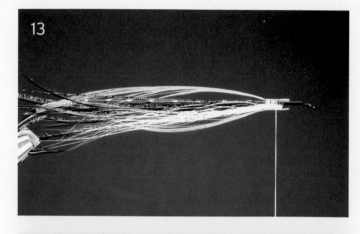

14. We're getting close to tying on the wings on the streamer. First, however, you'll want to tie on some sort of underwing base. This base will help support the wings when tying and fishing the fly. The underwing will also help keep the feather wings in position if the fly is mounted under glass.

A traditional method is to tie on a narrow bunch of bucktail for the underwing. This is an especially good method if you plan to fish with the fly; the bucktail will help keep the streamer swimming upright in the water. Be sure to use very straight hairs to tie a trim underwing; kinked hairs will make a thicker underwing and force the feather wings apart.

15. Mike Martinek, a talented streamer tier who lives in Massachusetts, showed me another way to make the base for the wing. Mike ties bunches of hackle fibers along the top of the hook shank. These fibers form a little bulk that helps support the front of the wings, but do not force the feathers apart.

Strip fibers from the same color of feathers used to make the wings. Tie on the first bunch of fibers right in front of the floss body.

16. Continue adding bunches of hackle fibers along the top of the hook shank. Stop before you reach the hook eye; be sure to leave ample room to tie on the wings.

17. Tie a bunch of gray hackle fibers on the bottom of the fly for a throat. The throat will hide all of the thread wraps you made to tie the body and underwing base.

18. It's time to change threads. Black thread is used to tie the head of the Gray Ghost, but you can select another color to tie a custom Ghost. I'm tying a very traditional Gray Ghost and will polish off the thread with black thread.

Start by tying off the white thread. You may use a whip finish, but a couple of half hitches will suffice. Next, start the black thread right in front of the white thread. Wrap the black thread back over the knot you made to tie off the white thread. Clip the white thread, and finish the fly with the black thread.

Now we're ready to tie on the wings. Read these instructions carefully and work slowly. Don't worry if things don't go well on the first try; you can always unwrap the thread and start again. (I'm a right-handed tier, and will describe the steps the way I tie a fly. If you're a lefty, proceed in an opposite manner).

Select the prepared wing that goes on the side of the fly that is facing you. Since I'm a right-handed tier, I'm facing the right side of the fly (as shown in the photograph). Place the wing in position against the side of the fly. The wing of the Gray Ghost is supposed to slightly veil the side of the fly, but note: I am not placing the wing on the exact side of the fly. Rather than placing the wing at the nine o'clock position (directly on the side of the hook shank), I am tying it on at the ten o'clock position (the reason for this will become clear in a moment). Hold the wing in place with your left thumb, grasp the bobbin of thread with your right hand, and make two or three light wraps of thread.

Place the second prepared wing on the far side of the fly at the two o'clock position. Hold the wing in place with your left index finger. Make another two or three light wraps of thread.

Adjust the wings until you are pleased with the appearance of the fly.

19. Here's a key to tying on the wings. Note that the wings of the fly are not parallel on the sides of the fly. Instead, the top edges of the wings are slightly touching, and the feathers form a sort of tall teepee; the top of the feathers press together to support the wings. Continue adjusting the feathers until you are pleased with the appearance of the wings.

20. When you are happy with the appearance of the fly, make three or four firm wraps of thread, and carefully clip the excess hackle stems. Apply a very small drop of superglue on top of the thread wraps.

21. Make a neat thread head, tie off the thread, and clip. Coat the head with cement.

Carrie Stevens applied a little band of red thread in the middle of the head of her Gray Ghost. A few tiers add this finishing touch to their flies, but I think that's going too far. That was her trademark—not mine—so I end with the all-black head. You can establish your own unique trademark by adjusting the proportions of the materials, or perhaps tying the head with a color other than black. Be creative and develop your own style!

22. Here's a classic Gray Ghost. A lot of folks seem mystified by this pattern, but as you can see, it's not that tough to tie. The key is to work slowly and carefully. Plan ahead while you work; think about the next step you'll have to make, and leave ample room to add the next group of materials. And remember that a few firm, well-placed wraps of thread do a better job than a bunch of thoughtless lashings of thread.

Chapter 4
Upright Feather Wings: Dressing the Chief Needahbah

The feather wings of the Gray Ghost are tied on the sides of the hook shank; the wings of the Chief Needahbah are tied on top of the hook. I had a tough time selecting a demonstration pattern for tying top-mounted wings—there are so many beautiful, fish-catching streamers—but this is one of my favorites.

The Chief Needahbah was developed by Chief Roland Nelson (aka Chief Needahbah). Roland Nelson was a member of the Penobscot tribe of Native Americans. He owned Needahbah's Shack, a tackle store in Greenville, Maine. This part of Maine is historic for its fine fishing. Greenville is located at the southern end of Moosehead Lake, and is less than a half-hour drive to the Roach River, the East Outlet of the Kennebec River, the Moose River, and numerous lakes and ponds. I've fished in this area many times, and I'm only beginning to scratch the surface. In addition to offering some of the finest fishing and best hospitality in the Northeast, the Greenville area is also the birthplace of many classic streamers.

Here's a recipe for the Chief Needahbah:

Hook: 6X-long streamer hook, sizes 6 to 2.
Thread: Black 6/0.
Tag: Flat silver tinsel.
Tail: A section of a goose or turkey quill dyed red.
Body: Red floss.
Rib: Flat silver tinsel.
Throat: Red hackle fibers, tied on the middle of the hook shank.
Wings: Yellow and red saddle hackles.
Cheeks: Jungle cock.
Collar: Red hackle.

TYING THE CHIEF NEEDAHBAH

1. Start the thread near the end of the hook shank. Tie on a piece of narrow silver tinsel.

2. Wrap the tinsel tag. Tie off and clip the excess tinsel. I have created a rather pronounced tag that starts opposite the tip of the barb and extends up the hook to a position opposite the hook point.

3. Clip a narrow strip from a goose, duck or turkey wing feather dyed red. You'll use this strip of feather to tie the tail of the fly.

4. Tie on the slip of red feather at the end of the hook shank to form the tail of the streamer. Tip: Pinch the feather strip against the hook shank, and make three or four firm wraps of thread. Pinching the strip against the hook prevents the feather from rolling around the shank when you wrap the thread and helps make a neater tail.

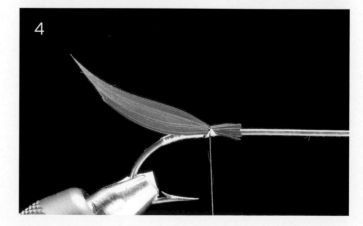

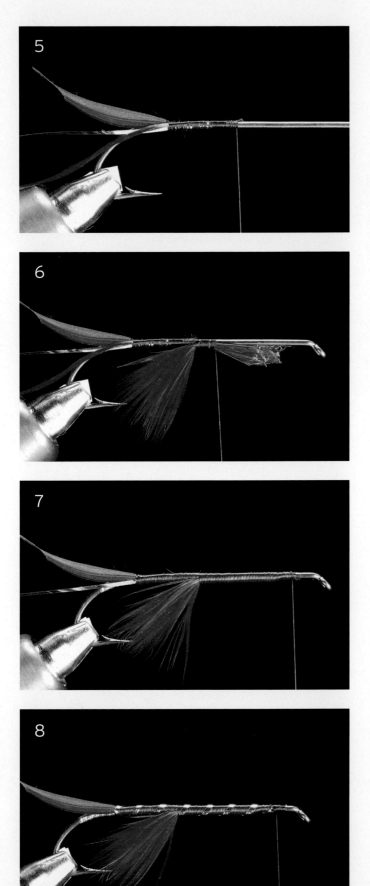

5. Tie on a piece of red floss and a piece of silver tinsel. The tag ends of these pieces of material should extend about half way up the hook shank. Wrap the thread up the hook, securing the tag ends along the top of the shank.

6. Strip a bunch of fibers from red hackle. Tie the fibers to the middle of the hook shank, forming a throat on the bottom of the hook. The butt ends of the fibers should extend to just behind the hook eye.

7. Wrap the floss up the hook shank. Pass the floss from hand to hand to prevent the material from twisting. If you place the floss in a bobbin and wrap the material like thread, occasionally spin the bobbin counterclockwise. This will prevent the floss from twisting tight.

Wrap the floss up the hook to directly behind the hackle-fiber throat; the floss should actually press against the base of the fibers. Wrap the floss in front of the throat; the first wrap should lie against the base of the fibers. Continue wrapping the front half of the floss body. Tie off and clip the excess floss.

8. Spiral-wrap the tinsel over the body to form the rib of the fly. Tie off and clip the surplus tinsel.

9. Make the wings of the Chief Needahbah following the steps we took for making the wings of the Gray Ghost. Each wing is made of a yellow hackle, a red hackle, and a jungle cock feather. Glue together feathers using thick head cement.

Place the prepared wings together. Position the wings on top of the hook, and make two or three light wraps of thread.

10. Adjust the wings until you are pleased with the appearance of the fly. The wings of the Chief Needahbah should be directly on top of the hook. Make three or four firm wraps of thread.

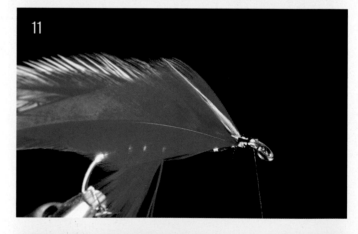

11. Tie a saddle hackle on the side of the fly. Secure the feather with firm wraps of thread.

12. Grasp the tip of the hackle in a hackle pliers. Pull the hackle taut. Fold the fibers down.

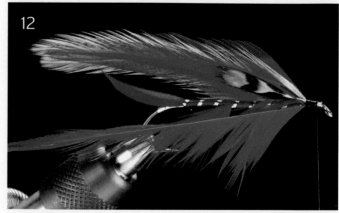

13. Wrap the hackle collar. Keep brushing back the fibers while you wrap the feather. Tie off and clip the excess hackle tip.

14. Brush back the hackle fibers. Make several firm wraps of thread at the base of the hackle collar.

15. Make a neat thread head. Clip the thread, and coat the head with cement. The Chief Needahbah is a beautiful pattern, and a good example of a streamer with wings tied on top of the hook.

Chapter 5
TYING TANDEM-HOOK STREAMERS

A lot of fly fishers look down their noses at tandem-hook streamers as representing an impure form of fly fishing. These patterns are something dirty and to be avoided. No self-respecting fly fisher, they will claim, would use such flies. But I'm not so sure. I haven't made up my mind.

This problem makes me ponder the question: what is fly fishing? Is it the act of casting in a certain manner, or does it have more to do with what we cast? What if I tether a bare hook to the end of my leader, impale a wiggling worm onto the hook, and cast the bait with a fly rod using the usual fly-casting method: am I fly fishing? Or what if I dangle a fly—made of tinsel, floss, hair and feathers—into the water with the aid of a baitcasting rod, or even just a long stick (the first fly-fishing rods, after all, were made of solid wood and were little more than long sticks)? I am fishing with a fly, but am I fly fishing?

Maybe this is too philosophical for a book about tying flies, or maybe it just doesn't matter. You fish the way you want to, and I'll fish the way I please. Each to

his own, as long as we don't violate the local fishing regulations.

If you like to troll the open lakes until the rivers warm and become more hospitable for wading, you'll want to tie tandem-hook streamers. We're going to examine three ways to dress tandem-hook streamers. The differences lie in the construction of the two-hook rigs that form the chassis of these flies. To be more specific, we'll examine different ways to cover the bare wire connecting the hooks. The first pattern is tied with a simple bare wire, which is the most common way to make these flies, and then we'll look at two easy ways to cover the wire.

TYING A BASIC TANDEM-HOOK STREAMER THE BLUE SAPPHIRE

Hooks: 2X-long streamer hooks, size 2.

Thread: Kevlar, size 3/0 or gel-spun thread for attaching the wire to the hook shanks, and black 6/0 for completing the fly.

Wire: 20- or 25-pound-test steel leader material.

Body: Flat silver tinsel.

Belly: Peacock herl and violet bucktail.

Wings: Purple hackles.

Shoulders: Kenyan guinea fowl.

Cheeks: Jungle cock.

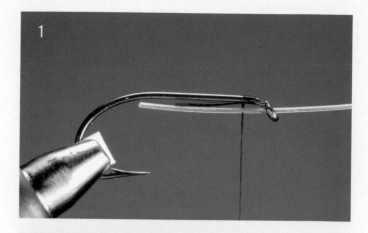

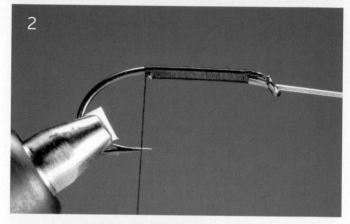

1. Let's start with making the trailing hook. Start a spool of Kevlar, size 3/0 or gel-spun thread near the hook eye. Slip a piece of wire into the hook eye. The wire should extend to the end of the hook shank.

2. Wrap the thread to the end of the wire. Use firm, closely spaced wraps of thread. Keep the wire positioned on the bottom of the hook shank.

3. Apply a drop of superglue to the thread wraps. The firm wraps of stout thread and superglue permanently lock the wire to the hook.

4. Tie a piece of silver tinsel to the end of the hook. Wrap the wire to the hook eye.

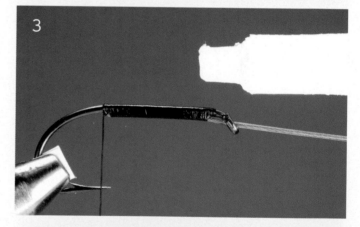

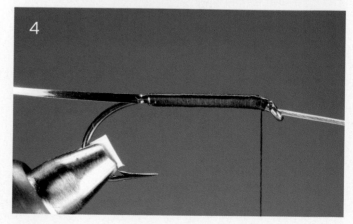

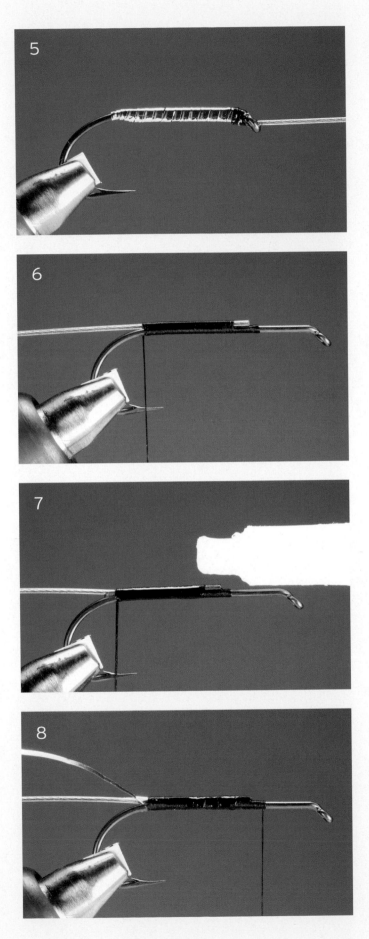

5. Wrap the tinsel up the hook to form the body. Tie off and clip the excess tinsel. Tie off the thread and clip. Coat the thread head with cement. This completes the stinger hook. Now we can turn to the front half of the fly.

6. Start the thread on the hook. Wrap a thread base on the hook shank. Place the end of the wire coming from the stinger hook on top of the shank. Note: I have placed the wire on the back two-thirds of the hook shank. Leave ample room on the front of the hook to tie on the body materials and wings. Bind the wire to the hook with firm wraps of thread.

7. Apply a drop of superglue to the thread wraps.

8. Tie a piece of silver tinsel to the end of the hook shank. Wrap the thread up the shank.

9. Wrap the tinsel up the shank to form the body on the front hook.

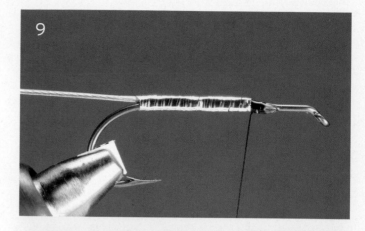

10. Here we see the completed tandem-hook rig. This is a very simple and efficient method for making these rigs. The combination of extra-strong thread and superglue makes indestructible connections. When you hook a fish, your tippet will snap—or your rod will break—long before the wire slips from the hooks.

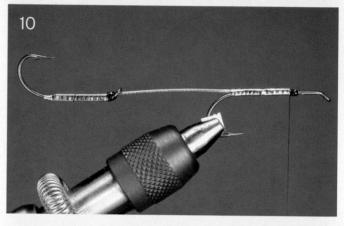

11. Now we can complete the fly. I left sufficient room between the hook eye and end of the body to tie on the belly material, throat, and underwing. For complete instructions, flip back to pages describing how to tie the Gray Ghost.

12. The completed Blue Sapphire. This is one of my patterns. It first appeared on the cover of the Autumn 1999 issue of *Fly Tyer* magazine. After that issue appeared, I received several letters from folks interested in tying this fly; one of the letters even came from Japan. There is a global interest in tying classic streamers.

TYING A TUBE TANDEM-HOOK STREAMER

This method features a tube placed on the wire connecting the hooks. The tube is dressed with the same materials used to tie the body on the hook shanks. Making this tube adds an extra step, but the body of the completed fly is more attractive. This might not matter to the fish, but it does to me. For this exercise we'll tie one of Carrie Stevens's patterns called the Tomahawk. Here's the pattern:

Hooks: 2X-long streamer hooks, size 2.
Thread: Kevlar, size 3/0 or gel-spun thread for attaching the wire to the hook shanks, and black 6/0 for completing the fly.
Wire: 20- or 25-pound-text steel leader material.
Tag: Flat silver tinsel.
Body: Red floss.
Rib: Flat silver tinsel.
Belly: Peacock herl and white bucktail.
Wings: Blue and red hackles.
Shoulders: Green golden-pheasant body feathers.
Cheeks: Jungle cock.

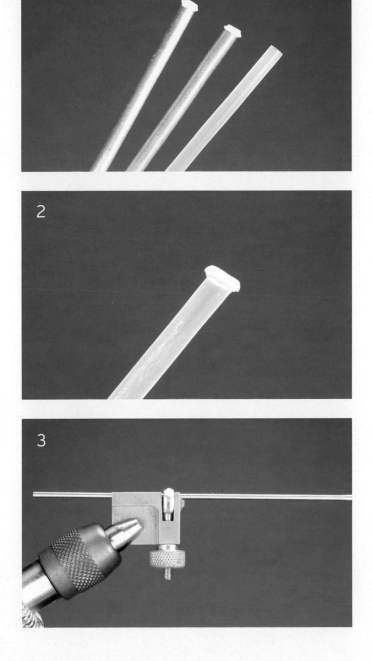

1. There are three types of tubes: plastic, aluminum, and brass. Tubes also come in several lengths. Use plastic tubes to make flies that troll shallow; use aluminum and brass tubes to tie streamers that troll deeper.

2. Cut the plastic tube to length; you'll need only enough tube to cover the bare wire connection between the two hooks. Lightly heat the ends of the tube; use just enough heat so the plastic rolls back and forms a ridge on each end of the tube. These ridges prevent the thread and floss from falling off the ends of the tube.

3. Several companies offer products for tying tube flies. One of the most convienent and affordable is the Tube Fly Tying Tool by HMH Vise. (You'll find their contact information in the appendix.) This tool fits almost all of the popular vises.

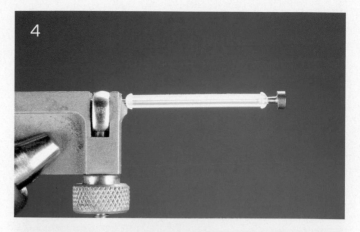

4. Slip the needle in the tube, and place the needle in the tool. Push the needle back until it binds the tube in place and will not rotate. Turn the brass screw on the bottom of the tool to lock the needle and tube in position. (The HMH Tube Fly Tying Tool comes with a complete set of instructions, as well as a selection of tubes.)

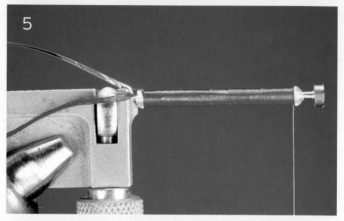

5. Start the thread on the tube. Tie on a piece of red floss and silver tinsel. Wrap the thread to the front of the tube.

6. Wrap the floss up the tube. Tie off and clip the excess floss. Wrap the tinsel rib. Tie off and clip the excess tinsel. Tie off the thread and clip. Coat the thread head with cement. This tube will make a nice transition between the trailing and forward hooks.

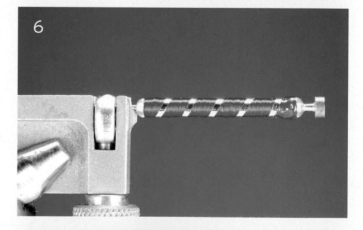

7. Now we're ready to tie the fly. Let's start with the trailing hook. Start the thread on the hook shank. Insert the wire into the hook eye. Bind the wire to the hook with firm wraps of thread. Apply a drop of superglue. Note that I wrapped the thread down into the hook bend; I did this so I can add a tinsel tag.

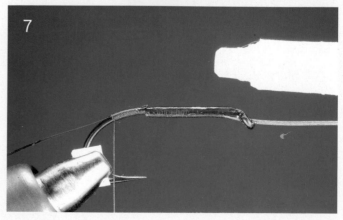

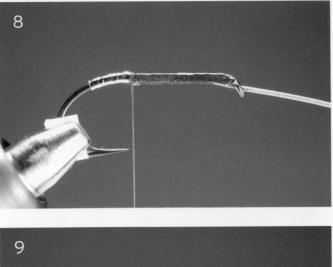

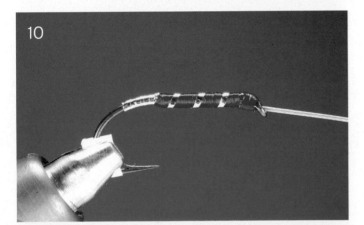

8. Tie on a piece of tinsel. Wrap the tinsel tag. Tie off and clip the excess tinsel.

9. Tie on a piece of red floss and piece of narrow silver tinsel.

10. Wrap the floss up the shank. Tie off and clip the surplus floss. Wrap the tinsel rib. Tie off and clip the excess tinsel. Make a neat thread head. Clip the thread, and coat the head with cement. This completes the trailing hook.

11. Slip the prepared tube on the wire. Tie the wire to the top of the hook shank; use firm wraps of thread, and coat the thread wraps with superglue. Tie on a piece of red floss and silver tinsel.

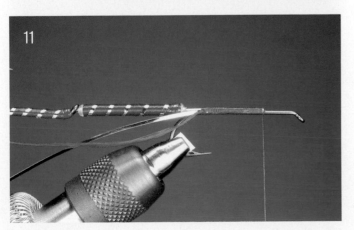

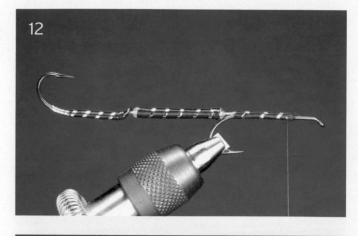

12. Wrap the floss up the hook shank. Tie off and clip the excess floss. Wrap the tinsel rib. Tie off and clip the surplus tinsel. Making a tube for a tandem-hook rig takes more time, but the results are gratifying. The tube really adds to the appearance of the finished fly.

13. Tie on the underwing, belly, and throat.

14. Tie on the wings to complete the Tomahawk.

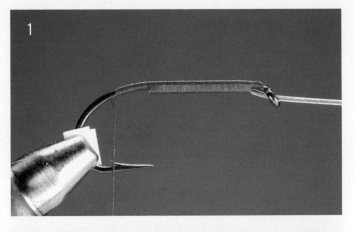

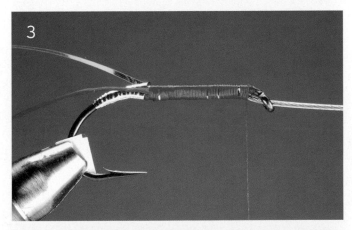

TYING THE BEAD TANDEM-HOOK STREAMER

Our last tandem pattern features beads slipped onto the wire connecting the two hooks. I like to use beads that replicate the colors of the body materials. While not an exact match, such as applying the materials to a tube, the beads do contribute to the appearance of the steamer. The bright silver beads also give the fly a little extra flash. For this example we'll tie Shang's Favorite, another of the famous Carrie Stevens patterns:

Hooks: 2X-long streamer hooks, size 2.
Thread: Kevlar, size 3/0 or gel-spun thread for attaching the wire to the hook shanks, and black 6/0 for completing the fly.
Wire: 20- or 25-pound-text steel leader material.
Body: Red floss.
Rib: Flat silver tinsel.
Belly: White bucktail.
Underwing: Peacock herl.
Wings: Grizzly hackles.
Shoulders: A duck or hen breast feather dyed red.
Cheeks: Jungle cock.

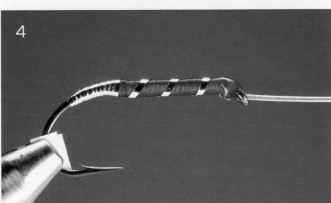

1. Start the thread on the hook. Slip a piece of wire into the hook eye. Bind the wire to the hook shank using firm wraps of thread. Place a drop of superglue on the thread wraps.

2. Tie on a piece of flat silver tinsel. Wrap the tinsel tag.

3. Tie on a piece of red floss and silver tinsel.

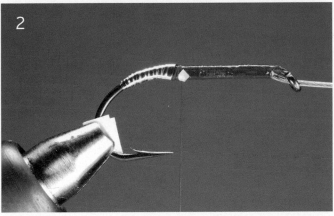

4. Wrap the floss up the shank to form the body on the stinger hook. Tie off and clip the floss. Wrap the tinsel tag. Tie off and clip the tinsel. Make a neat thread head. Tie off and clip the thread. Coat the thread head with cement.

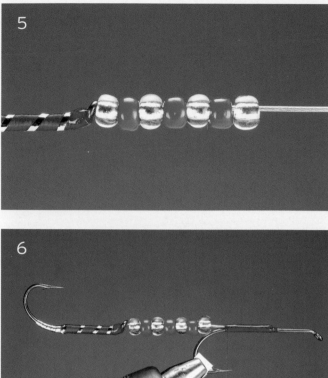

5. Slip beads on the wire. Use only enough beads to cover the wire between the stinger and forward hook.

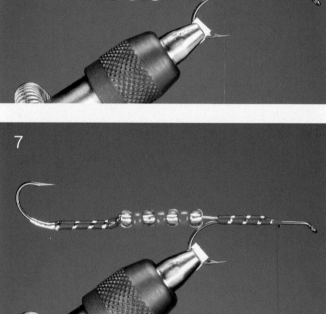

6. Position the forward portion of bare wire on top of the forward hook shank. Bind the wire to the shank using very firm wraps of thread. Coat the thread wraps with superglue.

7. Complete the body on the forward hook with red floss and flat silver tinsel. The beads help maintain the appearance of the body.

8. Tie on the underwing, belly, and throat of the streamer.

9. The completed tandem-hook Shang's Favorite.

Chapter 6
THE GRADUATE COURSE: TYING THE LADY DOCTOR

I think we're about to tie one of the most challenging flies in this book: the Lady Doctor.

In his book, *Streamer Fly Tying & Fishing*, Col. Joseph Bates calls this streamer the Lady Doctor Bucktail, but I think that's a mistake. First, of course, this fly contains no bucktail; the hairs in the underwing are black bear and polar bear. That would be splitting hairs (no pun intended) if the fly was tied like a bucktail, but it also has a wing made of large jungle cock feathers. I think Lady Doctor is a mixed-wing pattern, containing a combination of hair and feathers.

Joseph Stickney, of Saco, Maine, designed the Lady Doctor in 1926. Joe Stickney did not tie flies, but had the Percy Tackle Company, of Portland, Maine, do the honors. Just like with the Chief Needahbah, I contend that the Lady Doctor demonstrates the link between fancy Atlantic salmon flies and early freshwater streamers.

I am including the Lady Doctor as your graduation test for this course on tying streamers. If you can tie a nice Lady Doctor, you pass the course and are ready to tackle almost any freshwater streamer. Gook luck, and no cheating.

Here's the pattern for the Lady Doctor:

Hook: 6X-long streamer hook, size 6 or 4. (The length of the jungle cock feathers you have limits the size of the hooks you can use.)
Thread: White 6/0 for tying the body, and black 8/0 for completing the fly and making the head.
Tag: Flat silver tinsel.
Butt: Red floss.
Tail: Two yellow hackle tips.
Body: Yellow floss.
Ribs: Flat silver tinsel and a yellow hackle.
Underwing: Black-bear and polar-bear hair.
Wings: Jungle-cock feathers.
Shoulders: Hen or duck breast feathers dyed red.
Cheeks: Jungle cock.

DRESSING THE LADY DOCTOR

1. Start the thread on the end of the hook shank. Tie on a piece of narrow silver tinsel. Wrap the thread down into the bend of the hook, and then wrap it back up the hook to the point where the tinsel tag will end.

2. Wrap the tinsel up the hook to form the tag. Tie off and clip the excess tinsel.

3. Tying the tail is the next step. Start by selecting two yellow hackles. These hackles have nice even shapes and slightly rounded tips. They are perfect for making the tail.

4. Strip the excess fibers from the base of each hackle. I like a generous tail on this pattern, and leave enough feather so the completed tail is almost equal to the length of the body.

   Here's a tip to help you tie a nice tail. Strip a few fibers from the side of each feather that will lie against the hook. This will allow the tail to rest neatly against the hook.

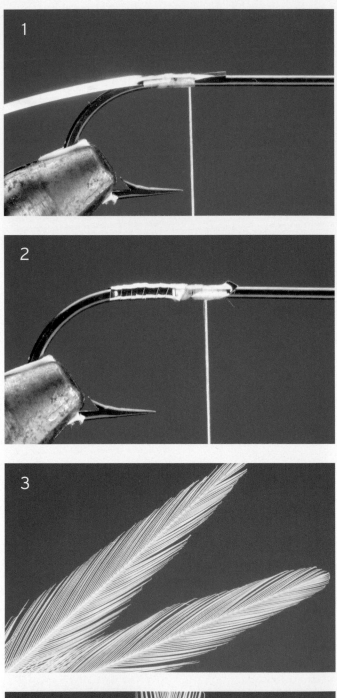

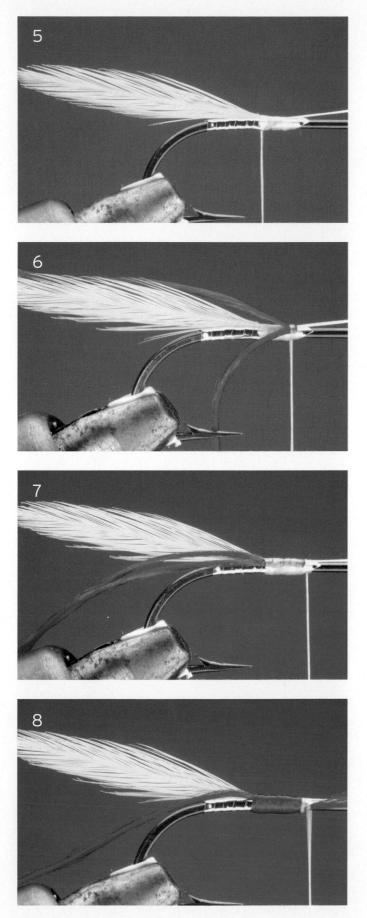

5. Place the tail feathers together. Position the feathers on top of the hook, and make two or three firm wraps of thread to secure the tail to the hook. Wrap the thread up the shank to form a smooth underbody for the butt.

6. I'm going to show you how to make a floss butt that won't slip down the hook when you fish the fly. I don't know if you'd really want to fish a Lady Doctor—the wings are made of jungle-cock feathers, which aren't exactly cheap—but this method is excellent for tying durable flies.

First, fold a strand of red floss around the thread. Make two firm wraps of thread.

7. Wrap the thread down to the base of the tail, securing the floss along the top of the hook shank. It is especially important that at least one of the strands of floss lay along the top of the shank. Wrap the thread back up the hook to the point where the butt will end.

8. Wrap one of the strands of floss up the shank to form the butt of the Lady Doctor. Tie off and clip the excess.

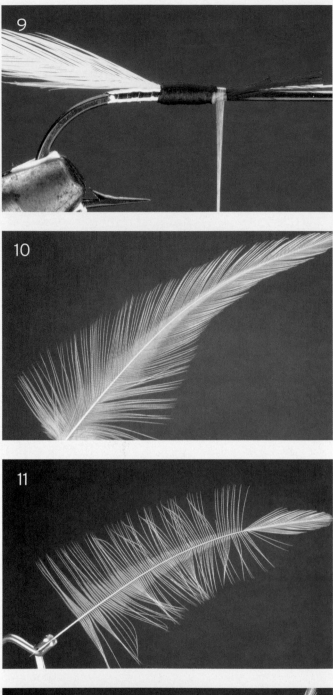

9. Fold the second strand of floss over the top of the butt. Make two gentle wraps of thread over the floss. Pull the floss forward, and pull the thread tight. Make another couple of firm wraps of thread, and clip the surplus floss.

The strand of floss that is folded forward locks the butt in place so that it doesn't slip down the hook when fishing.

10. Select the hackle for wrapping up the body of the fly. Here I have chosen a well-proportioned saddle hackle.

11. Strip the fluffy fibers from the base of the feather. Stroke the fibers out perpendicular to the hackle stem.

12. Fold the feather fibers so all of the fibers are on the same side of the hackle.

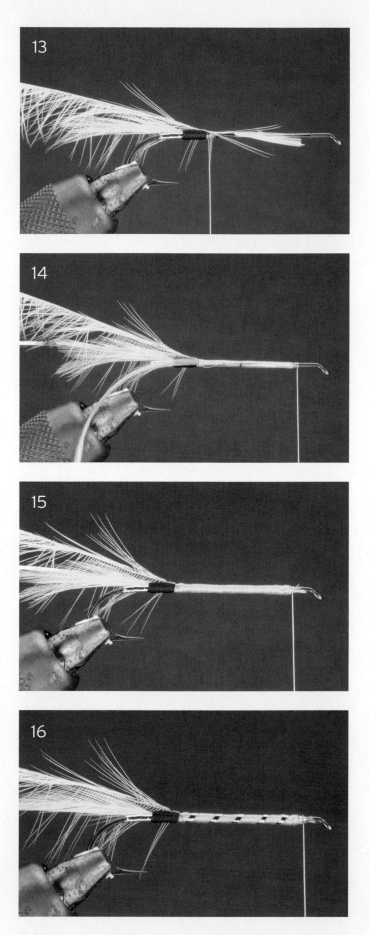

13. Tie the tip of the hackle in front of the floss butt. Do not clip the excess hackle tip; this will become part of the underbody and help make a smooth floss body.

14. Tie on a piece of yellow floss and narrow silver tinsel. Be sure to position the tinsel at the base of the folded hackle.

15. Wrap a smooth, level floss body. Tie off and clip the excess floss. Don't crowd the hook eye: leave ample room for tying on the wings.

16. Spiral-wrap the tinsel over the body to form the rib. Tie off and clip the excess tinsel.

17. Wrap the folded hackle up the body in front of the tinsel rib. Keep brushing back the hackle fibers while you work; the fibers should flow toward the end of the fly. Tie off the hackle. Clip the excess hackle tip only if you are pleased with the appearance of the hackle.

This is one of the most difficult steps of tying the Lady Doctor. Work slowly, and keep brushing back the hackle fibers. If things don't go well, just unwrap the hackle and start again. Don't clip the hackle tip until you are satisfied.

18. Strip a small bunch of yellow hackle fibers from another feather. Tie these on the bottom of the hook to form a throat and thicken the front of the streamer.

19. All of the hackle fibers on top of the hook shank will get in the way of tying on the wings. Clip those fibers using your sharpest scissors.

20. Clip a small bunch of black-bear hair from the hide, remove any underfur and short pieces of hair. Tie the bunch to the top of the fly using three firm wraps of thread.

The first layer of the underwing of a traditional Lady Doctor is black-bear hair. Keep in mind that a lot of black-bear hair is slightly kinky; I pawed through a lot of patches of hair until I found one that had the straight fibers shown in the photo. No harm is done if you substitute with bucktail dyed black or another black hair. This is especially true if you substitute with another material in the next tying step.

21. The second layer of the underwing is made of polar-bear hair. This material is available, but rather expensive. While a few synthetic materials come close to matching the natural sheen and transluscence of polar bear, no other natural material has these qualities. Keep in mind that while you can substitute with a synthetic material, these ingredients do not have the natural taper of real hair. If you must use a substitute, select bucktail or another natural hair, preferably something that matches the texture of the black hair.

Clip a small bunch of polar-bear hair from the pelt. Remove any underfur and short pieces of hair. Tie the bunch of white hair on top of the fly using two or three firm wraps of thread.

22. Sorry, but I don't know of a reasonable substitute for the long jungle-cock feathers used to tie the wings on the Lady Doctor. You'll find these feathers along the bottom edge of a jungle-cock cape. Each cape has only a few of these feathers, so they are precious. Select two of these feathers.

I will strip the fluffy fibers from the base of this feather so that it extends from the hook eye almost to the end of the underwing.

23. I glue together the feathers of each wing following the same method used to construct the wings for the Gray Ghost. Apply a small bead of thick head cement along the base of the jungle-cock feather, and press the red hen feather in place.

24. Place a small drop of thick cement on the back of the jungle-cock cheek. Position the jungle-cock feather in the middle of the hen feather. Press the feathers together, and allow the glue to dry.

25. Place the completed wings together. Set the wings on top of the hook, and make two or three loose wraps of thread. Adjust the wings until you are pleased with the appearance of the fly. Note that the red hen feathers slightly veil the body of the streamer. Use a bodkin needle to lift and set the hen feathers onto the sides of the fly. The hen feathers are pressing together over the top of this fly, and slightly flair out down the sides of the body.

When you are happy with the position of the wings, place a very small drop of superglue on the thread wraps and feather stems to lock the wings in place.

26. Make a neat thread head. Tie off the thread and clip. Coat the head with cement.

27. The Lady Doctor is my favorite freshwater streamer for admiring, if not fishing. It is my Exhibit A for proving that the designs of many classic freshwater streamers were inspired by colorful Atlantic salmon patterns. Once you master this pattern, you'll be able to tie any classic streamer.

Chapter 7
MARABOU STREAMERS: THE BALLOU SPECIAL

The Ballou Special is a different form of feather-wing streamer. Rather than using hackles, the most common wing material, the wing of the Ballou Special is made of marabou.

Marabou is a marvelous material. It is very soft, and gives the fly a lifelike swimming action in the water. All fly shops carry marabou; it comes in a rainbow of colors, and it is inexpensive.

The Ballou Special was first tied in 1921 by A.W. Ballou of Litchfield, Maine. Some tiers credit Ballou with having originated marabou streamers. These flies remain basically the same, and they still catch fish. This is what you'll need to dress the Ballou Special:

Hook: 6X-long streamer hook, sizes 6 to 2.
Thread: Black 6/0.
Tail: Two golden-pheasant crest feathers.
Body: Flat silver tinsel.
Underwing: Red bucktail.
Belly: Peacock herl and violet bucktail.
Wings: White marabou.
Topping: Peacock herl.
Cheeks: Jungle cock.

TYING THE BALLOU SPECIAL

1. Here we see a full golden-pheasant head with crests and tippet feathers. The crest feathers are the golden plumes on top of the head. Select two of these feathers to tie the tail of the Ballou Special.

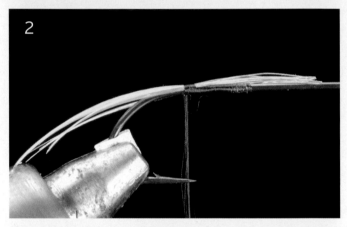

2. Start the thread at the end of the hook shank. Since the body of the Ballou Special is made of flat silver tinsel, I am tying the entire fly with black thread. Stack the golden-pheasant crest feathers. Tie the feathers to the end of the hook shank curving down.

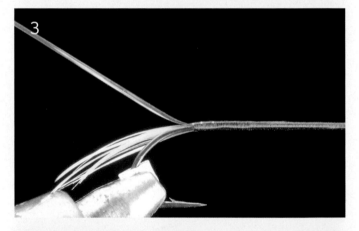

3. Tie a piece of silver tinsel to the end of the hook shank at the base of the tail. Wrap the thread up the shank.

4. Wrap the tinsel up the shank to form the body of the streamer. Tie off and clip the excess tinsel. Don't crowd the hook eye; be sure to leave ample room to tie on the wing.

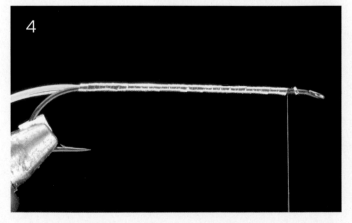

5. Tie on a small bunch of bucktail to form the underwing of the fly. The underwing of a traditional Ballou Special is made of red bucktail, but you can experiment and use other colors. Changing colors fundamentally alters the appearance of the fly in the water.

6. Here we see a fluffy marabou blood feather. The recipe for the Ballou Special given by Col. Bates in his book *Streamers and Bucktails* calls for two blood feathers, but I think this makes a thick and bulky wing. I prefer using only one marabou feather.

7. Lightly moisten the marabou feather (a little spit works wonders). Stroke the feather so all of the fibers are going in the same direction. Position the feather on top of the hook shank, and make two or three firm thread wraps.

8. Tie six to eight pieces of peacock herl on top of the wing.

9. Select two jungle-cock feathers. Strip the fluffy fibers from the base of each feather. Tie a feather on each side of the fly. I tie the jungle-cock feathers to angle up on the sides of the wing.

10. Wrap a neat thread head. Tie off and clip the thread. Coat the head with cement.

11. The completed Ballou Special is relatively easy to tie. It is also one of the most effective patterns you'll ever fish for large trout, salmon, and bass. Change the color of the wing and underwing to create a whole family of fish-catching flies.

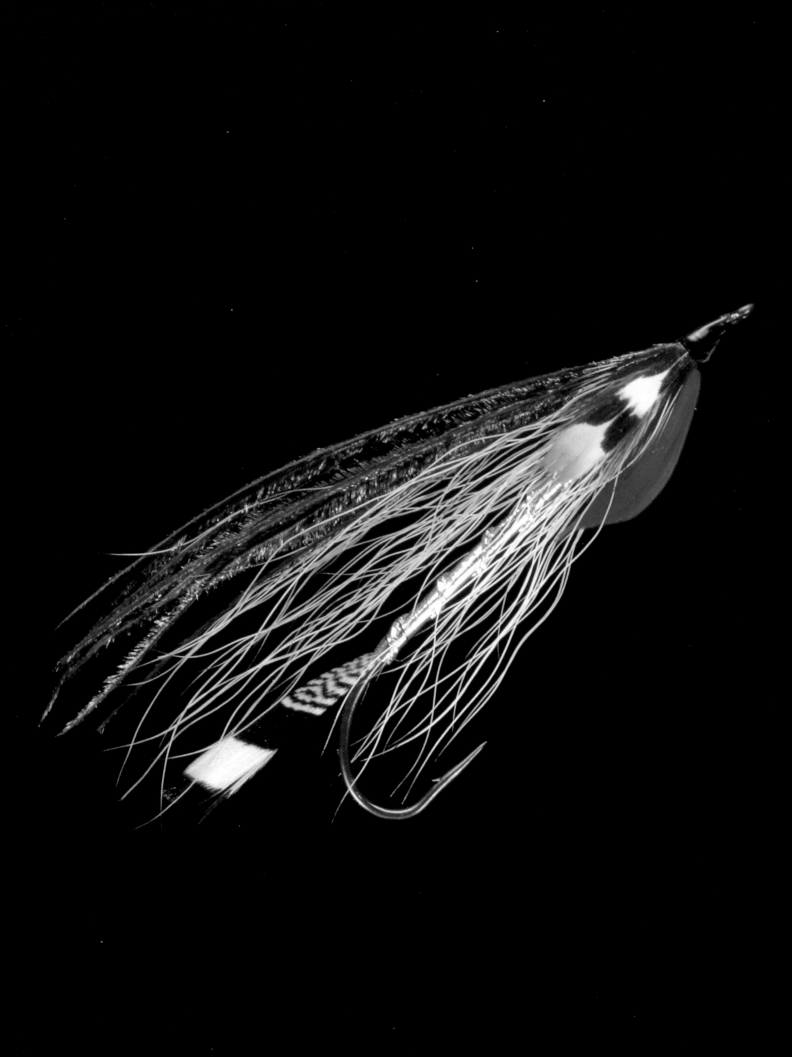

Chapter 8
TYING BUCKTAILS: THE GOVERNOR AIKEN

Bucktails have been among the favorite patterns of tens of thousands of fly fishers. These flies have universal appeal. They are easier to tie than the typical feather-wing streamer, are very durable, and the component materials are relatively inexpensive.

The name says it all: bucktails. The hair from deer tails is the main ingredient of these flies. The hair is used to make the wings, and the wings give the flies the silhouette of baitfish.

In a more generic sense, these patterns are sometimes called hair wings. Maybe that's a more accurate description because you can tie many of these flies using a wide variety of hairs: squirrel tail, bear, yak, and other hairs. There are also a wide variety of synthetic hairs that can be used to create lovely flies, although I suppose those materials have no place in a book about classic streamers (but they should have a place on your tying bench).

For our lesson on dressing a bucktail, I have selected a streamer called the Governor Aiken. This fly was named for Governor Aiken of Vermont. Surprisingly, Joe Bates does not offer the name of the designer in his otherwise very authoritative books. Regardless of who developed this pattern, it is an excellent imitation of a smelt, and is a popular streamer for catching landlocked salmon and trout. Learn to dress the Governor Aiken, and then substitute with other colors of bucktail—and other natural and dyed hairs—to create a variety of other patterns. Here's what you'll need to tie the Governor Aiken:

Hook: 4X- to 6X-long streamer hook, sizes 8 to 2. (The length of the hairs on the bucktails you use will determine the maximum hook size.)

Thread: Black 6/0.

Tail: A strip from a barred wood-duck flank feather.

Body: Flat silver tinsel.

Rib: Oval silver tinsel.

Belly: White bucktail.

Throat: A strip from a goose, duck, or turkey wing feather dyed red.

Wing: Lavender bucktail.

Topping: Peacock herl.

Cheeks: Jungle cock.

TYING THE GOVERNOR AIKEN

1. Start the Governor Aiken by selecting a wood-duck flank feather. This feather is a very good example. Clip a section of feather containing black and white bars.

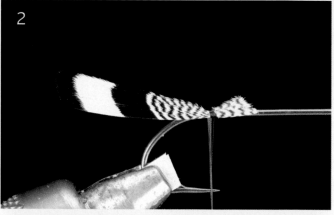

2. Start the thread at the end of the hook shank. Tie on the slip of wood-duck feather to form the tail.

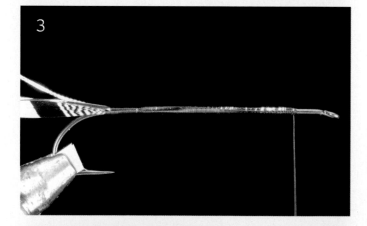

3. Tie on a piece of flat silver tinsel, and a piece of round silver tinsel. The excess tag of round tinsel should equal the length of the hook shank. Wrap the thread up the hook, securing the round tinsel tag along the top of the shank, creating a level underbody.

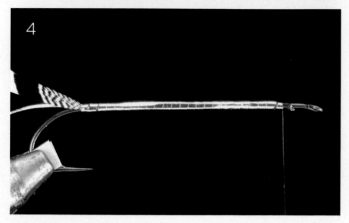

4. Wrap the flat tinsel body. Tie off and clip the excess tinsel.

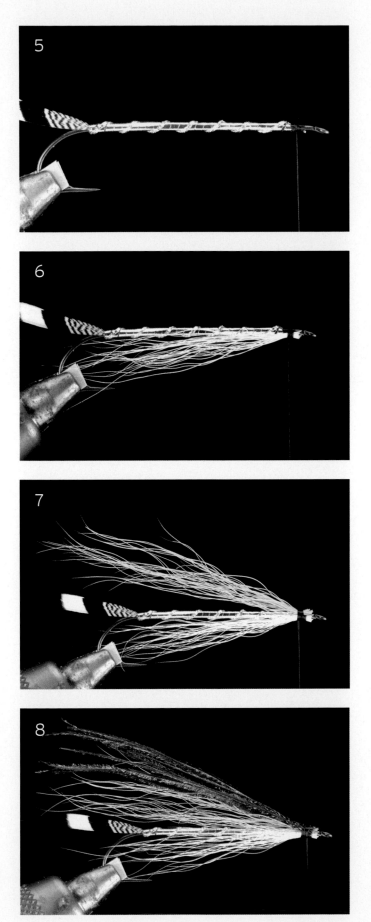

5. Spiral-wrap the round tinsel over the body to form the rib. Tie off and clip the excess tinsel. Try to tie off the round tinsel on the side of the fly so that it doesn't interfere with the bucktail wing or throat. (On this fly I tied off the tinsel on the far side of the fly.)

6. Clip a small bunch of white bucktail and remove any short hairs. Tie the bucktail on the bottom of the fly to form the belly of the streamer. I like the belly to extend into the bend of the hook.

7. Clip a bunch of violet bucktail and remove any short hairs. Tie the bucktail on top of the hook to form the wing.

8. Tie on six to eight pieces of peacock herl for the topping.

9. Clip a narrow slip from a duck or goose quill dyed red. Tie the slip on the bottom of the hook to form the throat of the fly. Secure the throat with two or three firm wraps of thread.

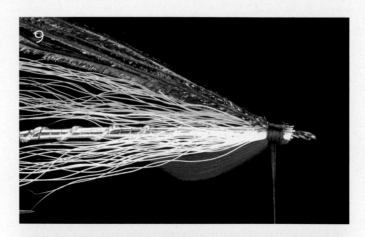

10. Select two jungle-cock feathers. Strip the fluffy fibers from the base of each feathers. Tie the jungle-cock feathers on each side of the hook to form the cheeks.

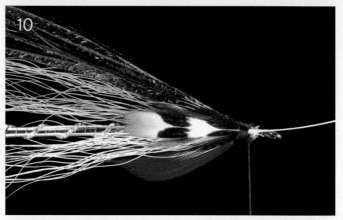

11. Wrap a neat thread head. Tie of the thread and clip. Coat the head with cement.

12. The completed Governor Aiken is an attractive bucktail. Use the pattern as the basis to dress other fish-catching streamers; experiment by changing the colors of bucktail used to make the wing and belly.

Chapter 9

A MODERN CLASSIC: THE THUNDER CREEK

or the life of me I don't know why I don't see more Thunder Creek–style streamers in the fly boxes of other anglers. These patterns are durable and do an excellent job of imitating small baitfish. Big fish eat little fish, and almost any freshwater trophy fish will eat a Thunder Creek (large pike and musky, which want large bait, are the only exceptions that come to mind).

According to the essay "A Brief History of the Thunder Creek Series," which appeared in Joe Bates's book *Streamer Fly Tying & Fishing* (Stackpole Books, 1995), Keith Fulsher tied the first members of the Thunder Creek Series in 1962. In 1972, he published his book, *Tying and Fishing the Thunder Creek Series* (Freshet Press). A few years later, he contributed articles to the first editions of *Fly Tyer* magazine in which he described new patterns and ways to dress Thunder Creeks.

A Thunder Creek is a unique way of tying a streamer. The key features are the wing and belly of the fly. Small bunches of bucktail are tied on the top and bottom of the hook with the tips pointing forward (out over the hook eye). The hairs are then pulled back and tied down to form the wing (the back), belly and head of the fly. You can change colors of bucktail to create new patterns. Fulsher used the Thunder Creek format to create an entire family of streamers designed to imitate specific baitfish—shiners, darters, minnows, trout, and bass—but you can also tie attractor-style Thunder Creeks. (Tip: In recent years, one of my favorite landlocked-salmon patterns has been an all-white Thunder Creek. This fly works all day, but is especially effective at dusk.)

Many members of the Thunder Creek family are about forty years old, and I consider them modern classics. Keeping with that theme, I'm going to show you how to tie an updated Thunder Creek Brown Trout. Rather than lacquering the head of the fly, as Keith did, I am going to use epoxy. And rather than painting the eyes, I am going to use adhesive Mylar eyes. I'm also going to add a few pieces of Krystal Flash to the wing to give the fly extra fish-attracting sparkle. Tie this fly and go catch some fish!

Hook: Straight-eye streamer hook, sizes 4 and 2.
Thread: Clear monofilament for tying the body, and red 6/0 for tying off the head.
Body: Gold-embossed tinsel.
Underwing: Red and black bucktail, mixed together and tied on top of the hook, and red Krystal Flash.
Belly: Yellow and white bucktail.
Wing: Brown bucktail.
Eyes: Small adhesive eyes.

TYING THE THUNDER CREEK

1. Start the monofilament thread near the end of the hook shank. Tie on a piece of gold-embossed tinsel.

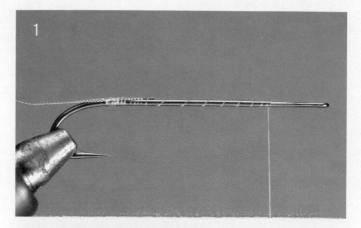

2. Wrap the tinsel up the hook shank to form the body.

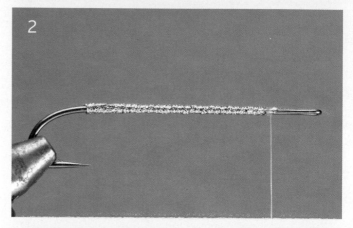

3. Mix together a few pieces of red and black bucktail. Tie the bucktail on top of the hook.

4. I'm tying a slightly modernized version of the classic Brown Trout Thunder Creek, and am adding four strands of red Krystal Flash to the underwing.

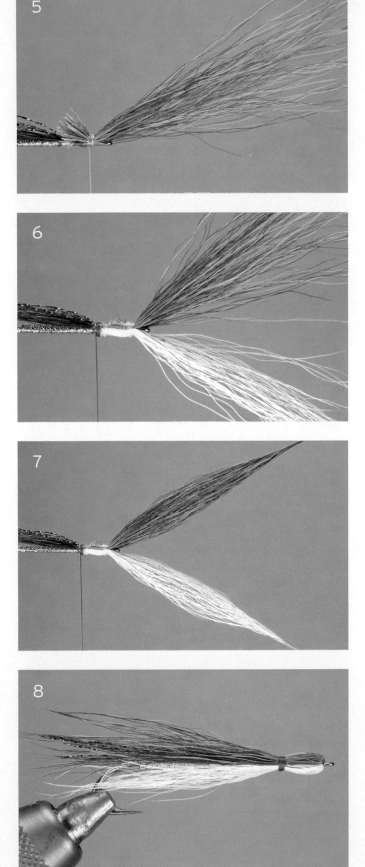

5. Clip a small bunch of natural brown bucktail. Remove any short hairs from the bunch, and even the tips. Tie the bucktail to the top of the hook with the tips pointing forward.

6. Mix together two very small bunches of white and yellow bucktail. Tie the bucktail on the bottom of the hook with the fibers pointing forward. Wrap the thread to the base of the underwing. Tie off the monofilament thread and clip. Start a spool of red thread.

7. You'll want to keep the bunches of bucktail separate when you fold the material back to form the wing and belly of the fly. It helps if you apply a dab of dubbing wax on the tip of each bunch. Lightly twist the hairs when you apply the wax. Don't get wax on the bucktail near the hook shank; the last step is to coat the head with epoxy, and the wax will prevent the glue from clinging to the hair.

8. Fold the bucktail back to form the wing and belly; make sure that the hairs cover the sides of the head. Make two or three wraps of thread. Pull the hair back to form a trim head, and tighten the thread. Make three more firm wraps of thread. Tie off the thread and clip.

9. Keith Fulsher covers the head of a Thunder Creek with two coats of varnish, and then paints an eye on each side of the head. I prefer using one coat of epoxy. Place an adhesive eye on each side of the head. Coat the head with five-minute epoxy.

10. The Brown Trout Thunder Creek is a modern classic. I altered the pattern with a few strands of Krystal Flash, adhesive eyes, and an epoxy head. This pattern is very durable, and has the streamlined silhouette of a baitfish.

Chapter 10
EVERYONE'S FAVORITE: THE MUDDLER MINNOW

Many fly fishers consider the Muddler Minnow an essential pattern for catching trophy trout, salmon, and bass. A Muddler Minnow forms the silhouette of a minnow or other baitfish when fished, and the head and collar "push" a lot of water and help the fish locate the fly.

The Muddler Minnow was developed by Don Gapen, of Anoka, Minnesota. At the time he was trying to create a fly to imitate the minnows inhabiting Ontario's Nipigon River, but today his pattern catches fish wherever freshwater anglers cast flies. The Muddler Minnow has become so important that it was featured on a U.S. postage stamp several years ago. If Don had incorporated his name in the name of the fly (perhaps Gapen's Minnow, sort of like Lefty's Deceiver or the Clouser Minnow), he would have become a very celebrated angler.

We're going to tie a traditional Muddler Minnow. The wings on this pattern are made of strips cut from a turkey tail feather. (Substituting marabou for the wing will give the fly additional fish-attracting action.)

Hook: 4X-long streamer hook, sizes 4 and 2.
Thread: I like to use Kevlar, but you can also use size 3/0 or one of the new gel-spun threads.
Tail: Mottled turkey.
Body: Flat gold tinsel.
Underwing: Gray squirrel tail hair.
Wings: Mottled turkey.
Head & collar: Deer hair, spun and clipped to shape.

TYING THE MUDDLER MINNOW

1. The tail and wings of the Muddler Minnow are made from strips cut from a turkey tail feather. This feather has lovely mottled markings, and will help give the pattern the natural appearance of a baitfish.

2. Clip a narrow strip from the turkey tail feather. Start the thread on the hook. Tie the strip to the end of the hook shank to form the tail of the fly. It might help if you pinch together the strip at the tie-in point. Do not clip the excess strip at this time; allow the excess to remain long and form a level underbody.

3. Tie on a piece of gold tinsel. Wrap the thread up the hook, binding the excess tail material to the hook shank. Do not wrap the thread to the hook eye; leave ample room—about one-third of the hook shank—to create the deer-hair Muddler-style head.

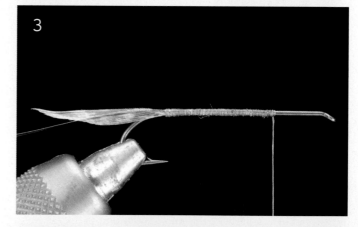

4. Wrap the tinsel up the hook shank to form the body of the fly. Tie off and clip the excess tinsel.

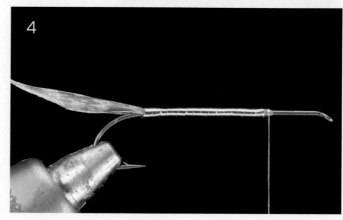

5. Clip a small bunch of gray squirrel-tail hair. Pick out any short fibers. Tie the remaining bunch of hair to the top of the hook shank to form the underwing.

6. Clip two narrow strips from a turkey tail feather; clip a strip from each side of the feather. Tie a strip onto each side of the squirrel tail hair to form the wing of the fly. Apply a drop of superglue on the thread wraps at the base of the wing.

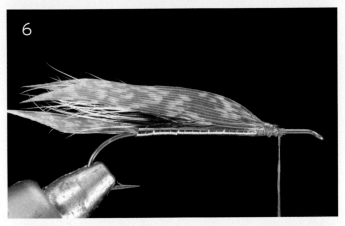

7. Now we're ready to make the head of the fly. Clip a bunch of deer hair about equal to the thickness of a pencil, maybe a bit bigger. Clean out any underfur from the base of the hair. At this point the tips of hair are uneven. Evening the tips is the first step in making a neat deer-hair collar. We'll do this in the next step.

8. Place the bunch of hair, tips first, in a hair stacker. Firmly tap the stacker on the top of your tying bench to even the tips.

9. Remove the hair from the stacker. Here we see the evened tips. This bunch will make a neat collar and head.

10. Hold the bunch of hair on top of the hook with the tips extending almost to the mid-point of the shank. Make two loose wraps of thread around the hook and over the hair. Tighten the thread. The hair will flair and spread around the hook. Release the hair and continue wrapping the thread. The key is to use very firm wraps of thread. Make three or four firm wraps of thread at the same spot.

The thread will eventually tighten, and the hair will stop spinning around the hook. Spread the hairs near the hook eye, and press the bunch back to the base of the wing. Tighten the thread again to secure the deer hair to the hook. Add another bunch of deer to the front of the hook shank. I usually use two bunches of hair to make the Muddler Minnow collar and head. Tie off and clip the thread. I prefer using a series of half-hitches, and apply a drop of superglue after I clip the thread.

11. Clip the head to shape. Work carefully; once you clip the hair off, you can't put it back. And take care not to clip the collar.

12. The Muddler Minnow is a modern classic streamer. Many anglers claim it is one of the most consistent producers of large fish. The deer-hair collar and head are a little difficult to tie, but with practice and determination, you'll get the hang of it.

Chapter 11

A GALLERY OF CLASSIC STREAMERS

*W*hat follows is a collection of more than 100 classic—and classically inspired—streamer patterns. I asked tiers to submit their favorite flies for this book. Several were good friends who I knew dressed great flies; others I knew only by their reputations as being expert tiers. Most consented and supplied me with flies. Many of the patterns were originally designed by other famous tiers, and just as many are original creations I know you'll want to tie.

This is the third book in which I've showcased the work of other tiers. In *Tying Contemporary Saltwater Flies* and *Guide Flies*, the flies of other tiers were major components.

(Guide Flies was entirely devoted to the patterns of working guides.) Why do I take this approach? It's not a question of being lazy; by the time I track down the addresses of all the tiers, write letters, send reminders, and field their phone calls and respond to their e-mail messages, I could just as easily tie the flies myself—and take all of the credit. I simply enjoy writing about what others are doing. It's more of a journalistic approach (not that I think writing about fly fishing is real journalism). I also think you enjoy seeing flies from as many tiers as possible.

Some of the following streamers are workmanlike "fish" flies, but many others are true works of art suitable for framing. All of the flies are excellent examples of classic freshwater streamers.

BIG BEN
designed by Carrie Stevens
tied by Selene Dumaine
Tag: Flat silver tinsel.
Body: Red floss.
Rib: Flat silver tinsel.
Belly: White bucktail.
Throat: Grizzly hackle fibers dyed yellow.
Underwing: A silver pheasant crest feather.
Wings: White and grizzly dyed yellow hackles.
Shoulders: Golden pheasant tippet feathers.
Cheeks: Jungle cock.

DEMON
designed by Carrie Stevens
tied by Selene Dumaine
Tag: Flat silver tinsel.
Body: Orange floss.
Rib: Flat silver tinsel.
Belly: White bucktail and peacock herl.
Wings: Grizzly hackles.
Shoulders: Lady Amherst pheasant tippet feathers.
Cheeks: Jungle cock.

WITCH

designed by Carrie Stevens
tied by Selene Dumaine
Tag: Flat silver tinsel.
Body: Orange floss.
Rib: Flat silver tinsel.
Belly: Peacock herl and white bucktail.
Throat: Grizzly hackle fibers.
Wings: Grizzly hackles.
Cheeks: Jungle cock.

PINK BEAUTY

designed by Carrie Stevens
tied by Selene Dumaine
Tag: Flat silver tinsel.
Body: Black floss.
Rib: Flat silver tinsel.
Belly: White bucktail.
Throat: Yellow hackle fibers.
Underwing: Peacock herl.
Wings: Pink hackles.
Shoulders: Lemon wood duck flank feathers.
Cheeks: Jungle cock.

GOVERNOR

designed by Carrie Stevens
tied by Selene Dumaine

Tag: Flat silver tinsel.
Body: Orange floss.
Rib: Flat silver tinsel.
Belly: White bucktail.
Throat: White hackle fibers.
Underwing: Peacock herl.
Wings: Grizzly dyed yellow and natural grizzly hackles.
Shoulders: Mallard duck shoulder feathers
    dyed brown.
Cheeks: Jungle cock.

GREEN BEAUTY

designed by Carrie Stevens
tied by Selene Dumaine

Tag: Flat silver tinsel.
Body: Orange floss.
Rib: Flat silver tinsel.
Belly: White bucktail.
Throat: A golden pheasant crest feather and white hackle
    fibers.
Underwing: Peacock herl.
Wings: Olive hackles.
Shoulders: Lemon wood-duck flank feathers.
Cheeks: Jungle cock.

DOCTOR GRAY

designed by Carrie Stevens
tied by Selene Dumaine
Tag: Flat silver tinsel.
Tail: Golden pheasant tippet fibers.
Body: Black floss.
Rib: Flat silver tinsel.
Throat: Pink hackle fibers.
Wings: Gray hackles.
Shoulders: Jungle cock body feathers.
Collar: Two or three wraps of a yellow hackle.

BLUE DEVIL

designed by Carrie Stevens
tied by Selene Dumaine
Tag: Flat silver tinsel.
Body: Flat silver tinsel.
Belly: White bucktail and peacock herl.
Throat: Orange and blue hackle fibers.
Wings: Orange and blue hackles.
Shoulders: Teal flank feathers.
Cheeks: Jungle cock.

CARRIE'S FANCY
designed by Carrie Stevens
tied by Selene Dumaine
Tag: Flat silver tinsel.
Body: Red floss.
Rib: Flat silver tinsel.
Throat: Blue hackle fibers.
Underwing: Peacock herl.
Wings: Pink hackles.
Shoulders: Mallard flank feathers.
Cheeks: Jungle cock.

QUEBEC WHORE
designed & tied by Ian Cameron
Body: White floss.
Rib: Flat silver tinsel over the white floss.
Underwing: Blue, white and red bucktail, followed by three
    pieces of pearl Flashabou.
Wing: Orange marabou.
Topping: Peacock herl.

WHITE GHOST
designed & tied by Ian Cameron
Tail: Yellow hackle fibers.
Body: Flat silver tinsel.
Rib: Oval silver.
Throat: Yellow hackle fibers.
Underwing: One piece of silver holographic Flashabou.
Wing: White marabou, flanked by a shorter piece of silver
   holographic tinsel on each side.

BLACK ICE
designed & tied by Ian Cameron
Tail: Red hackle fibers.
Body: Flat silver tinsel.
Rib: Oval silver tinsel.
Underwing: Lavender bucktail.
Wing: Black marabou.
Throat: Red hackle fibers.

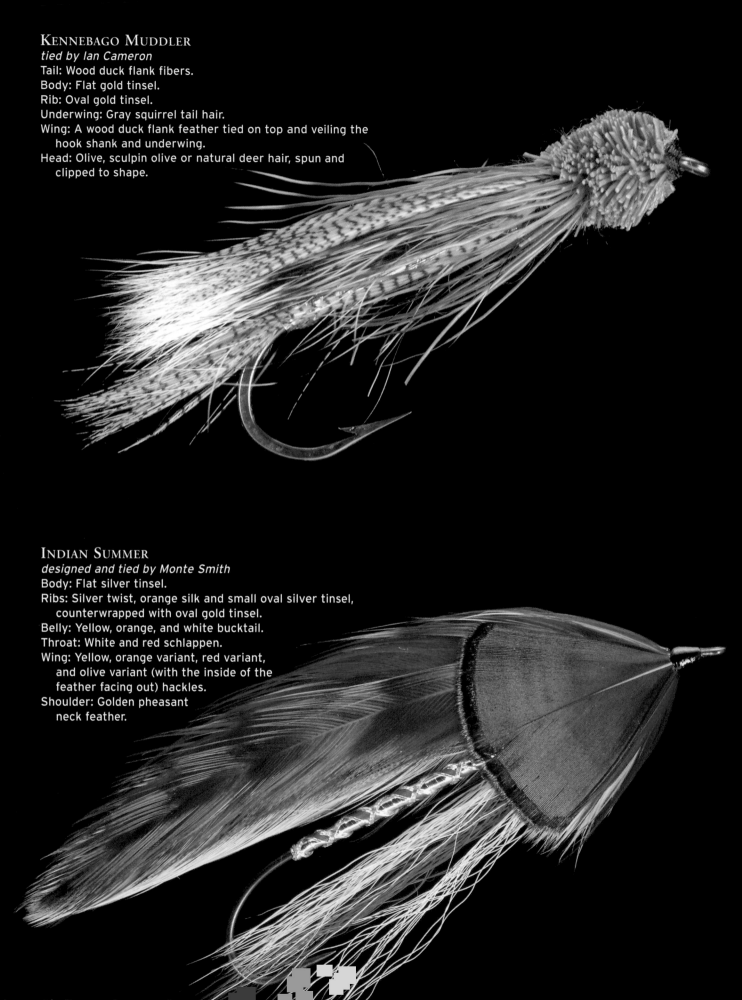

KENNEBAGO MUDDLER
tied by Ian Cameron
Tail: Wood duck flank fibers.
Body: Flat gold tinsel.
Rib: Oval gold tinsel.
Underwing: Gray squirrel tail hair.
Wing: A wood duck flank feather tied on top and veiling the
    hook shank and underwing.
Head: Olive, sculpin olive or natural deer hair, spun and
    clipped to shape.

INDIAN SUMMER
designed and tied by Monte Smith
Body: Flat silver tinsel.
Ribs: Silver twist, orange silk and small oval silver tinsel,
    counterwrapped with oval gold tinsel.
Belly: Yellow, orange, and white bucktail.
Throat: White and red schlappen.
Wing: Yellow, orange variant, red variant,
    and olive variant (with the inside of the
    feather facing out) hackles.
Shoulder: Golden pheasant
    neck feather.

SANTIAM SUNRISE

designed and tied by Monte Smith

Tag: Gold Body Braid.
Body: Purple floss.
Rib: Gold Body Braid.
Underwing: White and yellow bucktail.
Throat: White and deep red schlappen.
Underwing: Peacock herl covered with a
    golden pheasant crest feather.
Wing: Hot orange and purple
    hackles.
Shoulder: Mallard flank
    feathers dyed orange.
Cheeks: Jungle cock.

CARRIE'S FAVORITE

designed by Carrie Stevens
tied by Dr. G. S. "Stack" Scoville Jr.

Body: Flat silver tinsel.
Belly: White bucktail.
Throat: White hackle fibers and a golden pheasant crest
    feather.
Underwing: Peacock herl.
Wings: Magenta and golden badger hackles.
Cheeks: Jungle cock.

DON'S DELIGHT
designed by Carrie Stevens
tied by Bill Hrinko
Tag: Flat silver tinsel.
Tail: Red hackle fibers.
Body: Flat silver tinsel.
Throat: White hackle fibers.
Wings: White hackles.
Shoulders: Golden pheasant tippet feathers.
Cheeks: Jungle cock.

GENERAL MACARTHUR
designed by Carrie Stevens
tied by Bill Hrinko
Tag: Flat silver tinsel.
Tail: Red, white, and blue hackle fibers.
Body: Flat silver tinsel.
Throat: Red, white, and blue hackle fibers.
Wings: White, blue, and grizzly hackles.
Cheeks: Jungle cock.

Tag: Flat silver tinsel.
Body: Orange floss.
Rib: Flat silver tinsel.
Belly: White bucktail.
Throat: Grizzly hackle fibers.
Underwing: Peacock herl.
Wings: Grizzly hackles.
Shoulders: Golden pheasant
    tippet feathers.
Cheeks: Jungle cock.

GREYHOUND
designed by Carrie Stevens
tied by Bill Hrinko
Tag: Flat silver tinsel.
Tail: Red hackle fibers.
Body: Red floss.
Rib: Flat silver tinsel.
Belly: Peacock herl and white bucktail.
Throat: Red hackle fibers.
Wings: Gray hackles.
Shoulders: Jungle cock body feathers.
Cheeks: Jungle cock.

MORNING GLORY
designed by Carrie Stevens
tied by Bill Hrinko
Tag: Flat silver tinsel.
Body: Red floss.
Rib: Flat silver tinsel.
Belly: White bucktail.
Throat: Blue and black hackle fibers.
Underwing: A silver pheasant-crest feather.
Wings: Yellow hackles.
Shoulders: Red golden-pheasant
    body feathers.
Cheeks: Jungle cock.

WIZARD
designed by Carrie Stevens
tied by Bill Hrinko
Tag: Flat silver tinsel.
Body: Red floss.
Rib: Flat silver tinsel.
Belly: White bucktail.
Throat: White hackle fibers.
Underwing: Peacock herl.
Wings: Black and yellow hackles.
Cheeks: Jungle cock.

WEST BRANCH SPECIAL
designed and tied by Bill Hrinko
Body: Flat silver tinsel.
Belly: Polar bear hair.
Underwing: One golden-pheasant crest feather and peacock
   herl.
Wings: Gray and coq de Leon hackles.
Shoulders: Chukkar partridge.
Cheeks: Jungle cock.

MAGOG SPECIAL
designed and tied by Bill Hrinko
Tail: Teal flank fibers.
Body: Flat silver tinsel.
Throat: Red hackle fibers.
Wing: White, yellow, and purple bucktail.
Topping: Peacock herl.
Shoulders: Teal flank feathers.
Cheeks: Jungle cock.

MAGENTA MAIDEN
designed and tied by Bill Hrinko
Tag: Flat silver tinsel.
Body: Blue floss.
Rib: Flat silver tinsel.
Belly: Peacock herl and white bucktail.
Wings: Magenta hackles.
Topping: One golden-pheasant crest feather.
Shoulders: Chukkar partridge.
Cheeks: Jungle cock.

ORANGE DEMON
designed and tied by Bill Hrinko
Tail: Peacock sword fibers.
Body: Embossed copper tinsel.
Belly: Peacock herl and orange bucktail.
Wings: Orange and grizzly hackles.
Shoulders: Duck breast feathers dyed yellow.
Cheeks: Jungle cock.

SILVER DARTER VARIATION
designed and tied by Bill Hrinko
Tail: Peacock sword fibers.
Body: White floss.
Rib: Flat silver tinsel.
Belly: White bucktail and peacock sword fibers.
Wings: White variant hackles.
Shoulders: Small peacock feathers.

ADAMS
designed and tied by Bill Hrinko
Tail: Brown and grizzly hackle fibers.
Body: Gray hare's-ear dubbing.
Wings: Grizzly hackles.
Collar: Grizzly hen hackle with a brownish cast.

CHIEF
designed by Carrie Stevens
tied by Dr. G. S. "Stack" Scoville Jr.
Tag: Flat silver tinsel.
Tail: Red hackle fibers.
Body: Red floss.
Rib: Flat silver tinsel.
Throat: White hackle fibers.
Wings: Olive and brown hackles.
Cheeks: Jungle cock.

ROBIN
designed by Arthur Libby
tied by Libby's Flies
Body: Red floss.
Rib: Flat silver tinsel.
Wings: White, orange, green, and blue bucktail.
Topping: One strand of peacock herl.

SENATOR MUSKIE
designed by Arthur Libby
tied by Libby's Flies
Body: Red floss.
Rib: Flat silver tinsel.
Underwing: White, orange, and green bucktail.
Wings: Grizzly hackles.
Topping: Peacock herl.

HAZEL
designed by Arthur Libby
tied by Libby's Flies
Body: Flat silver tinsel.
Underwing: White and yellow bucktail.
Wings: Yellow and orange hackles.
Topping: Peacock herl.

GREEN WONDER
designed by Arthur Libby
tied by Libby's Flies
Body: Flat silver tinsel.
Underwing: White, yellow, and green bucktail.
Wings: Grizzly hackles.
Eyes: Red and white paint.

LIB'S SMELT
designed by Arthur Libby
tied by Libby's Flies
Body: Flat silver tinsel.
Throat: Red hackle fibers.
Wing: White, yellow, and purple bucktail.
Shoulders: Teal flank feathers.
Topping: Peacock herl.

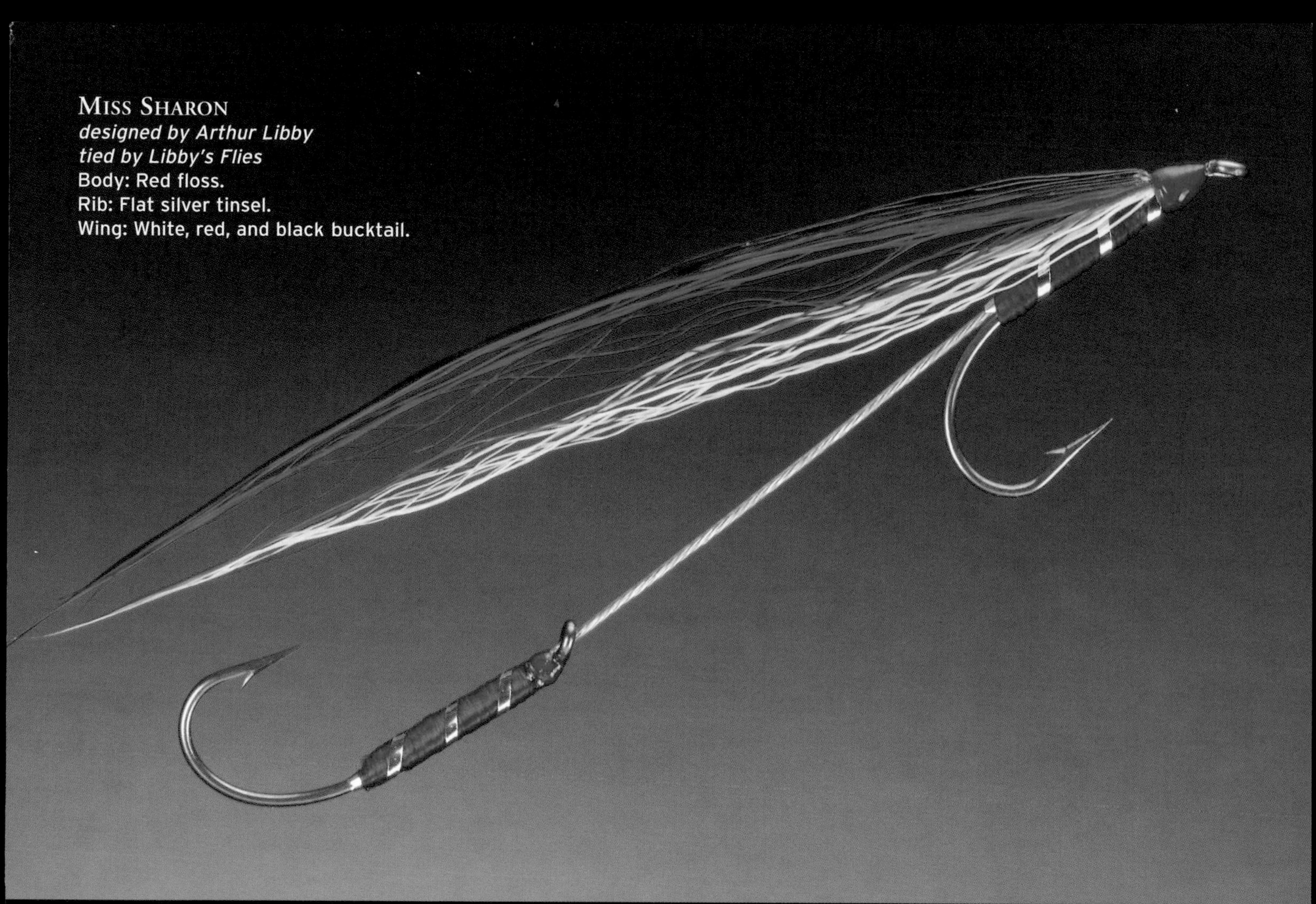

MISS SHARON
designed by Arthur Libby
tied by Libby's Flies
Body: Red floss.
Rib: Flat silver tinsel.
Wing: White, red, and black bucktail.

A. W. L.
designed by Arthur Libby
tied by Libby's Flies
Body: Red floss.
Rib: Flat silver tinsel.
Underwing: Red and yellow bucktail.
Wings: White hackles.
Topping: Peacock herl.

LIBBY'S CAL
designed by Arthur Libby
tied by Libby's Flies
Body: Red floss.
Rib: Flat silver tinsel.
Underwing: White bucktail.
Wings: Grizzly and grizzly dyed yellow hackles.
Shoulders: Silver pheasant body feathers.
Topping: Peacock herl.

RAIN
designed by Arthur Libby
tied by Libby's Flies
Body: Flat silver tinsel.
Underwing: Yellow and red bucktail.
Wings: Grizzly hackles.
Topping: Peacock herl.
Eyes: Red and white paint.

THE GOLD WONDER
designed & tied by Ed Wolfer
Tag: Flat gold tinsel.
Body: Embossed gold tinsel.
Rib: Oval gold tinsel.
Throat: Dark pink hackle.
Wings: Purple hackles.
Shoulders: Jungle cock.

KIM'S SPECIAL
designed & tied by Ed Wolfer
Tag: Flat gold tinsel.
Body: Dark blue floss.
Rib: Flat gold tinsel.
Belly: White bucktail and one golden pheasant crest feather.
Wings: Bright yellow and fire orange hackles.
Cheeks: Fairy blue bird and riffle bird.

BLACK MAX
designed & tied by Ed Wolfer
Tag: Oval silver tinsel.
Tail: Golden pheasant crest.
Butt: Black ostrich herl.
Body: Black floss.
Rib: Oval gold tinsel.
Throat: Tangerine hackle fibers.
Wings: Black hackles.
Shoulders: Jungle cock.

BLUEBACK
designed & tied by Charlie Mann
Body: Flat silver tinsel.
Belly: White bucktail.
Wing: Yellow, green, and blue bucktail.
Topping: Peacock herl.

CHAMPLAIN JANE
designed & tied by Charlie Mann
Body: Pearl Mylar tinsel.
Tail: The tag end of the body material.
Belly: Pearl Mylar tinsel, picked
    out and left long.
Wing: Purple bucktail.
Topping: Peacock herl.

MILLER'S SPECIAL
designed & tied by Charlie Mann
Body: Flat silver tinsel.
Belly: White and yellow bucktail.
Wing: Purple bucktail.
Topping: Peacock herl.

JOCK SCOTT BUCKTAIL
designed & tied by Charlie Mann
Body: Flat silver tinsel.
Belly: White bucktail.
Wing: Violet and red bucktail.
Topping: Peacock herl.

ONE-EYED POACHER
designed & tied by Bob Upham
Body: Embossed gold tinsel.
Underwing: Red bucktail.
Wing: Yellow bucktail.
Topping: A mallard flank feather folded over the top of the
    wing.
Eye: A red and yellow eye painted on one side of the thread
    head.

GOLDEN HEAD
designed & tied by Bob Upham
Tag: Flat gold tinsel.
Body: Black floss.
Rib: Flat gold tinsel.
Belly: White bucktail.
Wings: Brown hackles.
Shoulders: A golden pheasant tippet feather folded over the
    wing.

GRAND LAKER
designed & tied by Bob Upham
Tag: Flat gold tinsel.
Body: Black floss.
Rib: Two pieces of flat gold tinsel.
Belly: Black bucktail.
Throat: Brown hackle fibers.
Wings: Brown hackles.

TOMAH JOE
designed & tied by Bob Upham
Tail: Red and yellow hackle fibers.
Body: Flat silver tinsel.
Rib: Oval silver tinsel.
Throat: Light blue hackle fibers.
Wing: Teal flank fibers.
Topping: Peacock sword fibers.

WHOLLY GHOST
designed & tied by Bob Upham
Body: Flat silver tinsel.
Wings: Gray hackles.
Shoulders: Small mallard flank feathers.

THE RED DOG
designed & tied by Bill Chandler
Body: Rear two-thirds: flat copper tinsel. Front one-third: red
   wool dubbing.
Wings: Light blue and white variant hackles dyed red.
   (Variant hackles are feathers with unusual markings;
   in this case, the black tips and black edges at the bases.
   Variant hackles offer a creative tier a lot of opportunities
   to dress beautiful and unique patterns.)
Cheeks: Jungle cock.

SHELBURNE BAY SUNSET
designed & tied by Bill Chandler
Tail: Orange hackle fibers.
Body: Flat gold tinsel.
Belly: Orange, yellow, and white bucktail.
Wings: Yellow and orange hackles.
Shoulders: Any bright feather such as macaw, lorikeet, or
   parrot. (You may substitute any of these exotic feathers
   with a hen or duck breast feather dyed red.)
Cheeks: Jungle cock.

THE MS. BUSHAW
designed & tied by Bill Chandler
Tag: Flat silver tinsel.
Body: Green floss.
Rib: Flat silver tinsel.
Belly: White bucktail.
Wings: Claret and green hackles.
Shoulders: Francolin feathers.
Cheeks: Red broadbill feathers.

THE CONVERSE CREATURE
designed & tied by Bill Chandler
Tag: Silver holographic tinsel.
Body: Light olive floss.
Rib: Silver holographic tinsel.
Throat: Red and gray hackle fibers, top and bottom.
Wings: Silver pheasant crest, and golden olive, white, and light
    blue hackles.
Shoulders: Coral blue guinea fowl.
Cheeks: Jungle cock.

GRAY WOLF'S CORAL SMELT
designed & tied by Gray Wolf
Tag: Flat silver tinsel.
Tail: Orange hackle fibers.
Body: Light orange floss.
Rib: Flat silver tinsel.
Throat: Orange hackle fibers.
Wings: Tan and orange hackles.
Shoulders: Turquoise peacock breast
    feathers.
Cheeks: Jungle cock.

GRAY WOLF'S LLAMA HAIR "BROWN JULIE"
designed & tied by Gray Wolf
Tag: Embossed silver tinsel.
Body: White wool.
Rib: Embossed silver tinsel.
Wing: White bucktail and Foxtail-brown llama hair.
Topping: Copper AXXEL Flash.
Collar: Yellow hackle.

Tag: Flat silver tinsel.
Body: Light orange floss.
Rib: Flat silver tinsel.
Belly: Peacock herl, white bucktail, and a golden pheasant
    crest feather.
Throat: Red hackle fibers.
Wings: White hackles.
Shoulders: Ring-necked pheasant flank
    feathers.
Cheeks: Jungle cock.

GRAY WOLF'S BROWN SHADOW
designed & tied by Gray Wolf
Tag: Flat silver tinsel.
Tail: Orange hackle fibers.
Body: Light orange floss.
Rib: Flat silver tinsel.
Throat: Orange hackle fibers.
Wings: Light ginger dark brown hackles.
Cheeks: Jungle cock.

GRAY WOLF'S MIDNIGHT BLUE GHOST
designed & tied by Gray Wolf
Tag: Embossed silver tinsel.
Body: Red floss.
Rib: Embossed silver.
Belly: Peacock herl and white bucktail.
Throat: Orange hackle fibers.
Wings: Royal blue and black hackles.
Shoulders: Silver pheasant flank feathers.
Cheeks: Jungle cock.

GRAY WOLF'S SPIRIT OF '76
designed & tied by Gray Wolf
Tag: Flat silver tinsel.
Tail: Red, white, and blue hackle fibers.
Body: Red floss.
Rib: Flat silver tinsel.
Throat: Red, white, and blue hackle fibers.
Wings: Red and white hackles.
Cheeks: Jungle cock.

WOLF'S ICE-OUT SPECIAL
designed & tied by Gray Wolf
Tag: Flat silver tinsel.
Body: Light orange floss.
Rib: Flat silver tinsel.
Belly: Peacock herl, white bucktail, and a golden
    pheasant crest feather.
Throat: Red hackle fibers.
Wings: Silver gray and red hackles.
Shoulders: Mallard breast feathers
    dyed yellow.
Cheeks: Jungle cock.

WOLF'S DOCTOR'S WIFE
designed & tied by Gray Wolf
Tag: Embossed silver tinsel.
Body: Red floss.
Rib: Embossed silver tinsel.
Throat: Blue and yellow hackle fibers.
Wings: Kingfisher blue, red, and golden yellow
    hackles.
Shoulders: Mallard breast feathers
    dyed yellow.
Cheeks: Jungle cock.

WOLF'S D.K. SPECIAL
designed & tied by Gray Wolf

Gray Wolf says this pattern is "Named after
  David Klausmeyer in recognition of his fine contributions to the
  art of fly fishing." The author would like to thank him for his
  thoughtfulness.

Body: Purple UNI-Stretch.
Rib: Silver twist.
Belly: Peacock herl and white bucktail.
Throat: Black hackle fibers.
Wings: Black and grizzly hackles.
Shoulders: White Lady Amherst
  pheasant flank feathers.
Cheeks: Jungle cock.

GRAY WOLF'S LLAMA HAIR CHAPMAN'S SMELT
designed & tied by Gray Wolf

Hook: Mustad 3906B, size 4.
Body: Highlander green floss.
Rib: Silver twist.
Wing: Natural white llama hair mixed with pearl AXXEL Flash,
  gray dun llama hair mixed with black AXXEL Flash, and
  baitfish-green llama hair.
Topping: Rainbow AXXEL Flash.
Shoulders: Natural mallard breast feathers.
Cheeks: Jungle cock.

GRAY WOLF'S FLAMING BEAUTY
designed & tied by Gray Wolf
Tag: Flat silver tinsel.
Tail: Orange hackle fibers.
Body: Burnt orange floss.
Rib: Flat silver tinsel.
Throat: White, orange, and yellow hackle fibers.
Wings: White hackles.
Shoulders: Golden pheasant flank feathers.
Cheeks: Jungle cock.

WOLF'S RED GRAY GHOST
designed & tied by Gray Wolf
Tag: Flat silver tinsel.
Body: Red floss.
Rib: Flat silver tinsel.
Belly: Peacock herl, red bucktail, and a golden
   pheasant crest feather.
Wings: Gray and red hackles.
Shoulders: Silver pheasant body feathers.
Cheeks: Jungle cock.

GRAY WOLF'S PURPLE HAZE
designed & tied by Gray Wolf
Tag: Embossed silver tinsel.
Body: Flat gold tinsel.
Rib: Embossed silver tinsel.
Belly: Peacock herl, white bucktail, and fuschia bucktail.
Throat: Black hackle fibers.
Wings: Each wing is made of one black hackle
    flanked by a pink hackle, and then
    flanked by a shorter black hackle.
Cheek: Jungle cock.

GRAY WOLF'S QUEEN OF THE LAKE
designed & tied by Gray Wolf
Tag: Embossed silver tinsel.
Body: Light orange floss.
Rib: Embossed silver tinsel.
Belly: Peacock herl and white bucktail.
Throat: White hackle fibers and a golden pheasant
    crest feather.
Wings: White hackles.
Cheeks: Jungle cock.

SUPERVISOR
designed by Carrie Stevens
tied by Garret Booth
Tail: Red hackle fibers.
Body: Flat silver tinsel.
Rib: Oval silver tinsel.
Belly: White bucktail.
Throat: White hackles fibers.
Underwing: Peacock herl.
Wings: Light blue saddle hackles.
Shoulders: Pale green
    shoulder hackles.
Cheeks: Jungle cock.

DIVINITY
designed & tied by Garret Booth
Body: Pearl Mylar tinsel.
Tag: Red thread.
Belly: Polar-bear hair.
Underwing: A golden pheasant crest feather.
Wings: Gray hackles.
Shoulders: Gold tipped Lady
    Amherst pheasant
    feathers tied over mallard
    flank feathers.
Cheeks: Jungle cock.

FURSHORT'S LURKER
designed & tied by Garret Booth
Body: Silver holographic tinsel.
Belly: White bucktail.
Throat: Red schlappen fibers.
Wings: Olive hackles.
Shoulders: Silver pheasant body feathers.
Cheeks: Jungle cock.

GOLDEN DEMON
*designed & tied by Garret Booth (Adapted from
 the original Golden Demon pattern.)*
Tail: A golden pheasant crest feather.
Body: Gold Mylar tinsel.
Throat: Orange schlappen fibers.
Wings: Brown hackles.

THE PAVLIK
designed & tied by Garret Booth
Tag: Silver holographic tinsel.
Body: Light blue floss.
Rib: Silver holographic tinsel.
Belly: Peacock herl and gray bucktail.
Wings: Silver Doctor blue and grizzly dyed
    Silver Doctor blue hackles.
Shoulders: Blue back feathers from a
    ring-necked pheasant rooster, and
    guinea fowl feathers.
Cheeks: Green head feathers from
    a ring-necked pheasant rooster.

GRAY EYE
designed & tied by Mike Martinek, Jr.
Tag: Flat copper tinsel.
Body: Red floss.
Rib: Flat copper tinsel.
Belly: White bucktail and a golden pheasant crest feather.
Throat: White hackle fibers.
Underwing: Jungle cock feathers and peacock herl.
Wings: Red and gray hackles.
Shoulders: Lemon wood duck breast feathers.
Topping: Red hackle fibers.
Cheeks: Jungle cock.

CHARTREUSE GHOST
designed & tied by Mike Martinek Jr.
Tag: Flat silver tinsel.
Body: Red floss.
Rib: Flat silver tinsel.
Belly: Yellow and white bucktail, and a golden pheasant crest feather.
Throat: Yellow hackle fibers.
Underwing: Peacock herl.
Wings: Chartreuse hackles.
Shoulders: Silver pheasant body feathers.
Topping: Yellow hackle fibers.
Cheeks: Jungle cock.

MIKE'S RED GHOST SPECIAL
designed & tied by Mike Martinek Jr.
Tag: Flat silver tinsel.
Body: Red floss.
Rib: Flat silver tinsel.
Belly: Red bucktail and a golden pheasant crest feather.
Throat: Red hackle fibers.
Underwing: Peacock herl.
Wings: Red and gray hackles.
Shoulders: Silver pheasant body feathers.
Cheeks: Jungle cock.

ISLANDER
designed & tied by Mike Martinek Jr.
Tag: Flat silver tinsel.
Body: Red floss.
Rib: Embossed silver tinsel.
Belly: Orange, chartreuse, and white bucktail, and a jungle
cock crest feather.
Throat: Orange, dark pink, and bright blue hackle fibers.
Underwing: Peacock herl.
Wings: Orange and dark pink hackles.
Shoulders: Chartreuse guinea
fowl feathers.
Topping: Bright blue
hackle fibers.
Cheeks: Jungle cock.

FRYES LEAP
designed & tied by Mike Martinek Jr.
Tag: Flat silver tinsel.
Body: Orange floss.
Rib: Flat silver tinsel.
Belly: White bucktail.
Throat: Yellow, pale red, and light blue hackle fibers.
Underwing: Peacock herl.
Wings: White and pale red hackles.
Shoulders: Violet guinea fowl feathers.
Topping: Light blue hackle fibers.
Cheeks: Jungle cock.

ELECTRIC PERCH
designed & tied by Mike Martinek Jr.
Body: Flat silver tinsel.
Rib: Oval silver tinsel.
Belly: Chartreuse and white bucktail.
Throat: Yellow and pink hackle fibers.
Underwing: Peacock herl.
Wings: Chartreuse grizzly hackles.
Shoulders: Lemon wood-duck flank feathers.
Topping: Pink hackle fibers.
Cheeks: Jungle cock.

ORANGE DRAGON
designed & tied by Mike Martinek Jr.
Body: Flat silver tinsel.
Rib: Oval silver tinsel.
Belly: Yellow and white bucktail.
Throat: White and light blue hackle fibers.
Underwing: Orange bucktail.
Wings: Variant hackles (splashed with black mottling) dyed orange.
Shoulders: Lemon wood-duck flank feathers.
Topping: Light blue hackle fibers.
Cheeks: Jungle cock.

MIDNIGHT SUN
designed & tied by Mike Martinek Jr.
Tail: Golden pheasant crest feather.
Body: Flat copper tinsel.
Rib: Oval copper tinsel.
Belly: Orange bucktail.
Throat: Orange and yellow hackle fibers.
Wings: Badger dyed orange and violet hackles.
Shoulders: Lemon wood-duck flank feathers.
Topping: Orange hackle fibers.
Cheeks: Jungle cock.

DUN WANDERER
designed & tied by Mike Martinek Jr.
Tag: Flat silver tinsel.
Body: Red floss.
Rib: Flat silver tinsel.
Belly: Chartreuse and white bucktail, and a golden pheasant
    crest feather.
Throat: Red hackle fibers.
Underwing: Peacock herl and a golden pheasant
    crest feather.
Wings: Gray and violet hackles.
Shoulders: Lemon wood-duck
    flank feathers.
Topping: Yellow hackle fibers.
Cheeks: Jungle cock.

WINNI PINNI
designed & tied by Mike Martinek Jr.
Tail: Golden pheasant crest feather.
Body: Pearl Mylar tinsel.
Throat: Red calftail.
Underwing: Pink bucktail.
Wings: Badger hackles dyed blue.
Cheeks: Jungle cock.

INDIAN POND SPECIAL
designed & tied by Mike Martinek Jr.
Tail: Golden pheasant crest feather.
Body: Flat copper tinsel.
Rib: Copper wire.
Throat: Red hackle fibers.
Underwing: Violet and red bucktail.
Wings: Pale violet hackles.
Cheeks: Jungle cock.

BRAVE AMERICAN
designed & tied by Mike Martinek Jr.
Tail: Golden pheasant crest feather.
Body: Embossed silver tinsel.
Rib: Oval silver tinsel.
Belly: Red bucktail.
Throat: White and blue hackle fibers.
Underwing: White hackle fibers.
Wings: Blue grizzly hackles.
Topping: White and red
   hackle fibers.
Cheeks: Jungle cock.

JIM WARNER SPECIAL
designed & tied by Mike Martinek Jr.
Tail: Orange floss.
Body: Flat silver tinsel.
Rib: Oval silver tinsel.
Throat: Red hackle fibers.
Underwing: Yellow bucktail.
Wings: Olive grizzly hackles.
Cheeks: Jungle cock.

GUIDES SPECIAL
designed & tied by Henry Northridge
Body: Flat silver tinsel.
Belly: Light blue bucktail.
Underwing: Red bucktail.
Wing: Yellow hackles.

MERRYMEETING SPECIAL
designed & tied by Henry Northridge
Tail: A section of a goose or turkey feather dyed red.
Body: Red floss.
Rib: Flat silver tinsel.
Belly: Orange bucktail.
Underwing: White bucktail and peacock herl.
Wings: Grizzly hackles dyed yellow.
Cheeks: Jungle cock.

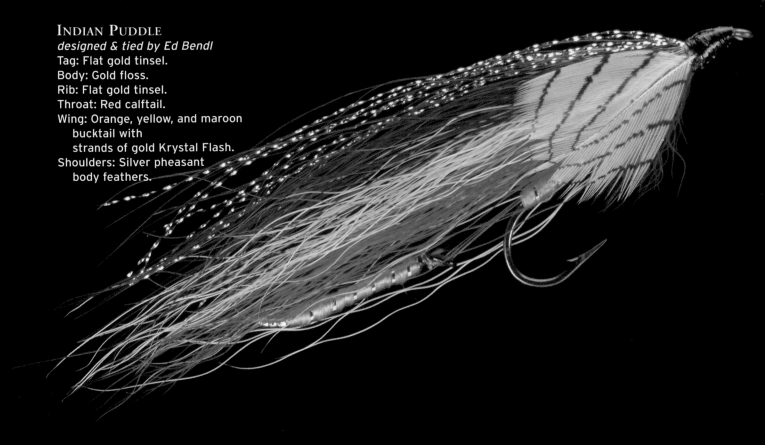

INDIAN PUDDLE
designed & tied by Ed Bendl
Tag: Flat gold tinsel.
Body: Gold floss.
Rib: Flat gold tinsel.
Throat: Red calftail.
Wing: Orange, yellow, and maroon
bucktail with
strands of gold Krystal Flash.
Shoulders: Silver pheasant
body feathers.

WEST CANADA
designed & tied by Ed Bendl
Body: Embossed silver tinsel.
Wing: White, green, and orange bucktail.
Topping: Peacock herl.
Shoulders: Brown ring-necked pheasant body feathers.

GOLDEN DARTER
designed by Lew Oatman
tied by Dick Talleur
Tail: A section of brown mottled turkey feather.
Body: Yellow floss.
Rib: Flat gold tinsel.
Throat: A small tip of a jungle-cock body feather.
Wings: Golden badger hackles.
Cheeks: Jungle cock.

SHUSHAN POSTMASTER
designed by Lew Oatman
tied by Dick Talleur
Tail: A section of brown mottled turkey feather.
Body: Light yellow floss.
Rib: Flat gold tinsel.
Throat: A few fibers from a duck wing quill dyed red.
Wing: Fox-squirrel tail hair.
Cheeks: Jungle cock.

BABY BROOK TROUT

designed by Lew Oatman
tied by Dick Talleur

Tail: White, black hackle, and orange hackle fibers.
Body: The first three-quarters is white floss, the final one-quarter is salmon-pink floss.
Rib: Flat gold tinsel.
Throat: White, black hackle, and orange hackle fibers.
Wings: Grizzly hackles dyed olive, and painted with alternating yellow and scarlet dots, three of each color along the quill.
Cheeks: Jungle cock.
Head: Olive thread painted white underneath.

SHANG'S SPECIAL

designed by Carrie Stevens
tied by Ed "Muzzy" Muzeroll

Body: Flat silver tinsel.
Belly: White bucktail.
Throat: White hackle fibers.
Underwing: Peacock herl.
Wings: Jungle cock feathers.
Shoulders: Duck breast feathers dyed red.
Cheeks: Jungle cock.

THE ENTICER
designed & tied by Ed "Muzzy" Muzeroll
Tag: Flat gold tinsel.
Body: Red wool yarn.
Rib: Flat gold tinsel.
Throat: Brown hackle fibers.
Wing: White and black bucktail.

MOOSEHEAD SMELT—SPRING
designed & tied by Ron McKusick
Tail: Yellow hackle fibers.
Body: Rear: flat silver tinsel. Front: fire orange thread,
    size 6/0.
Throat: Yellow hackle fibers.
Underwing: White bucktail and pearl Krystal Flash.
Wings: Purple and coq de Leon
    Pardo hackles.
Cheeks: Jungle cock

MOOSEHEAD SMELT—SUMMER
designed & tied by Ron McKusick
Tail: Yellow hackle fibers.
Body: Rear: flat silver tinsel. Front: fire orange thread,
    size 6/0.
Throat: Yellow hackle fibers.
Underwing: White bucktail and Krystal Flash.
Wings: Medium olive hackle and brownish coq
    de Leon Pardo hackle.
Cheeks: Jungle Cock Eye

MOOSEHEAD SMELT—FALL
designed & tied by Ron McKusick
Tail: Yellow hackle fibers.
Body: Rear: flat silver tinsel. Front: fire orange thread,
    size 6/0.
Throat: Yellow hackle fibers.
Underwing: White bucktail and pearl Krystal Flash.
Wings: A hot orange hackle flanked by a
    medium coq de Leon Pardo hackle.
Cheeks: Jungle cock.

LAC TERNAY SPECIAL
designed & tied by Ron McKusick
Tail: Golden pheasant tippet.
Body: Flame orange chenille.
Rib: Oval gold tinsel.
Underwing: Pearl Krystal Flash.
Wing: Two white marabou feathers.
Topping: Peacock herl
Shoulders: Mallard breast feather dyed
    hot orange.
Cheeks: Jungle cock.

GOVERNOR BARROWS
designed & tied by Ron McKusick
Body: Woven silver tinsel tied down with red thread and
    cemented.
Belly: White bucktail.
Throat: Yellow hackle fibers.
Underwing: Mixed red and blue bucktail.
Wings: Tan or wheat colored hackles.
Shoulders: Silver pheasant body feathers.
Cheeks: Jungle cock.

BARRED ORANGE PINK LADY
designed & tied by Ron McKusick
Body: Flat silver tinsel
Belly: White bucktail.
Throat: Yellow hackle fibers.
Underwing: Fine peacock herl taken from the
    top of a peacock eye.
Wings: Grizzly dyed hot orange hackles.
Shoulders: Lemon wood-duck.
Cheeks: Jungle cock.

ALLIE'S FAVORITE
designed by Carrie Stevens
tied by Dr. G. S. "Stack" Scoville Jr.
Tag: Flat silver tinsel.
Body: Red floss.
Rib: Flat silver tinsel.
Belly: White bucktail.
Throat: Orange and black hackle fibers.
Underwing: Peacock herl.
Wings: Orange and black
    hackles.
Cheeks: Jungle cock.

ARTULA
designed by Carrie Stevens
tied by Dr. G. S. "Stack" Scoville Jr.
Tag: Flat silver tinsel.
Tail: Orange hackle fibers.
Body: Orange floss.
Rib: Flat silver tinsel.
Belly: White bucktail.
Throat: Brown hackle fibers.
Wings: Green and black hackles.
Cheeks: Jungle cock.

ALLIE'S DELIGHT
designed by Carrie Stevens
tied by Dr. G. S. "Stack" Scoville Jr.
Tag: Flat silver tinsel.
Tail: Yellow hackle fibers.
Body: Flat silver tinsel.
Belly: White bucktail.
Throat: Yellow hackle fibers.
Underwing: Peacock herl.
Wings: White and grizzly hackles.
Cheeks: Jungle cock.

BLUE DEVIL
designed by Carrie Stevens
tied by Dr. G. S. "Stack" Scoville Jr.
Tag: Flat silver tinsel.
Body: Red and black floss.
Rib: Flat silver tinsel.
Belly: White bucktail.
Throat: Orange and black hackle fibers.
Underwing: Peacock herl.
Wings: Orange and blue hackles.
Shoulders: White and brown
    barred ruffed grouse
    body feathers.
Cheeks: Jungle cock.

BLUE DRAGON
designed by Carrie Stevens
tied by Dr. G. S. "Stack" Scoville Jr.
Tag: Flat silver tinsel.
Tail: Yellow hackle fibers.
Body: Flat silver tinsel.
Throat: Yellow hackle fibers.
Wings: Gray, blue, and grizzly hackles.
Cheeks: Jungle cock.

AMERICA
designed by Carrie Stevens
tied by Dr. G. S. "Stack" Scoville Jr.
Tag: Flat silver tinsel.
Tail: White hackle fibers.
Body: Flat silver tinsel.
Throat: White hackle fibers.
Wings: White, red, and blue hackles.
Cheeks: Jungle cock.
Head: Red, white, and blue thread.

CANARY
designed by Carrie Stevens
tied by Dr. G. S. "Stack" Scoville Jr.
Tag: Flat silver tinsel.
Tail: Black hackle fibers.
Body: Flat silver tinsel.
Belly: Yellow bucktail.
Throat: Yellow hackle fibers.
Wings: Yellow hackles.
Cheeks: Jungle cock.

CANARY—CUSTOM
designed by Carrie Stevens
tied by Dr. G. S. "Stack" Scoville Jr.
Tag: Flat silver tinsel.
Body: Orange floss.
Rib: Flat silver tinsel.
Belly: Yellow bucktail.
Throat: Yellow hackle fibers.
Wings: Yellow hackles.
Cheeks: Jungle cock.

CARRIE'S SPECIAL
designed by Carrie Stevens
tied by Dr. G. S. "Stack" Scoville Jr.
Body: Flat silver tinsel.
Belly: White bucktail.
Throat: White bucktail and one golden pheasant crest feather.
Underwing: One golden pheasant creast
    feather.
Wings: Pink and golden badger hackles.
Shoulders: Lady Amherst pheasant rump
    feathers.
Cheeks: Jungle cock.

CASABLANCA
designed by Carrie Stevens
tied by Dr. G. S. "Stack" Scoville Jr.
Tag: Flat silver tinsel.
Tail: Red hackle fibers.
Body: Flat gold tinsel.
Belly: White bucktail.
Throat: Red hackle fibers.
Wings: White and dark violet hackles.
Cheeks: Jungle cock.

CHARLES E. WHEELER
designed by Carrie Stevens
tied by Dr. G. S. "Stack" Scoville Jr.
Tag: Flat silver tinsel.
Body: Red floss.
Rib: Flat silver tinsel.
Belly: White bucktail.
Throat: White hackle fibers.
Underwing: Peacock herl.
Wings: Four gray hackles.
Shoulders: Each shoulder is made from
    one teal flank feather and one duck
    or hen breast feather dyed red.
Cheeks: Jungle cock.

Purveyors of Streamer Materials

The following suppliers offer fine materials for dressing streamers and other fine flies.

HUNTER'S ANGLING SUPPLIES
One Central Square, New Boston, New Hampshire 03070, 1-800-331-8558.

ANGLER'S WORKSHOP
P.O. Box 1910, Woodland, Washington 98674, (360) 225-9445.

CASTLE ARMS
P.O. Box 30070, Springfield, Massachusetts 01103, 1-800-525-4866.

GAELIC SUPREME HOOKS
P.O. Box 176, Wyncote, Pennsylvania 19095, (215) 886-7211.

COMPLETE SPORTSMAN
P.O. Box 826, Westborough, Massachusetts 01581, (508) 898-2990.

ENGLISH ANGLING TRAPPINGS
11 East Main Street, Pawling, New York 12564, (845) 855-5182.

THE SERIOUS FISHERMAN
East 10704 19th Avenue, Spokane, Washington 99206, 1-800-347-4654.

FLYTYERVARIANT.COM
flytyervariant.com.

HMH VISE
14 Main Street, Brunswick, Maine 04011, 1-800-335-9057

Bibliography

Remarkably few books have been written about freshwater streamers.
The following books, however, offer great insights into this fascinating family of flies.

Streamers & Bucktails: The Big Fish Flies
by Joseph D. Bates Jr. (Knopf: New York) 1980.

Streamer Tying & Fishing
by Joseph D. Bates Jr. (Stackpole Books: Mechanicsburg, PA) 1995.

Carrie Stevens: Make of Rangeley Favorite Trout and Salmon Flies
by Graydon and Leslie Hilyard (Stackpole Books: Mechanicsburg, PA) 2000.

Lost Flies
by Paul Schmookler and Igrid Sils (Complete Sportsman: Westborough, Massachusetts) 2000.

List of Featured Tiers
GREAT STREAMER DRESSSERS

The following lady and gentlemen provided beautifully dressed flies for this book. I would like to extend my heart-warmed thanks to them, and tip my hat to their expertise and creativity. With this list of names I am including the contact information they provided to me.

ED BENDL
Ed's Fly Shop
Route 30, Box 271
Northville, New York 12134
(518) 863-4223

GARRET BOOTH
98 Webster Highway
Temple, New Hampshire 03084
(603) 924-2396
albienut@prodigy.net

IAN CAMERON
354 Holden Road
Glenburn, Maine 04401
(207) 942-2522
ripgorge@hotmail.com

BILL CHANDLER
P. O. Box 5391
Burlington, Vermont 05402

SELENE DUMAINE
782 Main Street
Readfield, Maine 04355
(207) 685-3343

BILL HRINKO
136 Lionshead Drive E
Wayne, New Jersey 07470
(973) 831-0469

LIBBY'S FLIES
537 River Road
Standish, Maine 04084
(207) 642-2462
www.maine-crafts.com

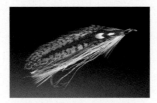

RON McKUSICK
Featherside Flies
663 Airport Road
Corinna, ME 04928
(207) 924-3886, ronmcq59@yahoo.com

CHARLIE MANN
345 Main Street
Winthrop, Maine 04364
(207) 377-2108

MIKE MARTINEK JR.
3 Florence Street
Franklin, Massachusetts 02038
(508) 528-6649

Ed "Muzzy" Muzeroll
22 Troy Trail
Sidney, Maine 04330
(207) 547-3927

HENRY NORTHRIDGE
4 Woburn Abbey Drive
Bedford, New Hampshire 03110
(603) 472-3769

HENRY "STACK" SCOVILLE
138 Prospect Hill
Nashville, Tennessee 37205
(615) 463-8721
FLYTYER-1@msn.com

MONTE SMITH
P. O. Box 532
Halsey, Oregon 97348

DICK TALLEUR
www.dicktalleur.com

BOB UPHAM
General Delivery
Grand Lake Stream, Maine 04637

GRAY WOLF
P. O. Box 641
Oquossoc, Maine 04964
www.streamerfliesbygraywolf.com

ED WOLFER
46 Mohawk Drive
Unionville, Connecticut 06085
(860) 675-5917

Index

A

Adams, 101
Allcock hooks, 15
Allie's Delight, 139
Allie's Favorite, 138
America (fly), 141
American Rooster, 18
Angora wool, 17
Artula, 139
A.W.L., 105

B

Baby Brook Trout, 134
Ballou Special, The, 10, 63–67
Barred Orange Pink Lady, 138
Basic Tandem-Hook Streamer,
   41–44
Bates, Joseph, 15, 23, 53, 69,
   75, 144
Bead Tandem-Hook Streamer, 49–51
Bendl, Ed, 145
   Indian Puddle, 132
   West Canada, 132
Big Ben, 88
Black Ice, 93
Black Max, 108
Black-bear hair, 20
Blue Devil, 91, 140
Blue Dragon, 140
Blue Sapphire, The, 41–44
Blueback, 108
Booth, Garret, 122, 145
   Divinity, 122
   Furshort's Lurker, 123
   Golden Demon, 123
   The Pavlik, 124
Brave American, 130
Brown Shadow, 116
Brown Trout Thunder Creek, 75–79
Bucktails, 1, 19–20, 69. *See also*
   specific flies

C

Cameron, Ian, 145
   Black Ice, 93
   Kennebago Muddler, 94
   Quebec Whore, 92
   White Ghost, 93
Canary, 141

Canary-Custom, 142
Candy's Smelt, 116
Carrie's Fancy, 92
Carrie's Favorite, 95
Carrie's Special, 142
Casablanca, 143
Castle Arms, 15, 16, 144
Champlain Jane, 109
Chandler, Bill, 145
   The Converse Creature, 114
   The Ms. Bushaw, 114
   The Red Dog, 113
   Shelburne Bay Sunset, 113
Charles E. Wheeler, 143
Chartreuse Ghost, 125
Cheeks, 10
Chenille, 16, 17
Chief, 102
Chief Needahbah, 35–39
Classic Gray Ghost, 23–33
   materials for, 23
   tying, 26–33
   wings, 23–26
Converse Creature, The, 114
Coral Smelt, 115

D

Demon, 88
Divinity, 122
D.K. Special, 119
Doctor Gray, 91
Doctor's Wife, 118
Don's Delight, 96
Dumaine, Selene, 146
   Big Ben, 88
   Blue Devil, 91
   Carrie's Fancy, 92
   Demon, 88
   Doctor Gray, 91
   Governor, 90
   Green Beauty, 90
   Pink Beauty, 89
   Witch, 89
Dun Wanderer, 128
Dyed hackles, 18

E

Electric Perch, 127
Enticer, The, 135

F

Feathers, 10, 18–19
Flaming Beauty, 120
Flosses, 17
Fryes Leap, 126
Fulsher, Keith, Thunder Creek, 75–79
Furs, 19–20
Furshort's Lurker, 123

G

Gaelic Supreme Hooks, 15, 16, 144
Gapen, Don, 81
General MacArthur, 96
Gold Wonder, The, 107
Golden Darter, 133
Golden Demon, 123
Golden Head, 111
Golden pheasant, 5, 19
Golden Witch, 97
Governor, 90
Governor Aiken, 69–73
Governor Barrows, 137
Grand Laker, 111
Gray Eye, 124
Gray Ghost. *See also* Classic Gray
   Ghost
Gray Wolf's Brown Shadow, 116
Gray Wolf's Coral Smelt, 115
Gray Wolf's D.K. Special, 119
Gray Wolf's Doctor's Wife, 118
Gray Wolf's Flaming Beauty, 120
Gray Wolf's Ice-Out Special, 118
Gray Wolf's Llama Hair "Brown
   Julie," 115
Gray Wolf's Llama Hair Chapman's
   Smelt, 119
Gray Wolf's Midnight Blue Ghost,
   117
Gray Wolf's Orange Tiger, 2
Gray Wolf's Purple Haze, 121
Gray Wolf's Queen of the Lake, 121
Gray Wolf's Red Gray Ghost, 120
Gray Wolf's Spirit of '76, 117
Green Beauty, 90
Green Wonder, 104
Greyhound, 97
Guides Special, 131
Guinea fowl, 8

H

Hackles, 3, 18
Hair wings, 10, 69. *See also*
  Bucktails
Hairs, 19–20, 69
Hazel, 103
HMH Vise, 45, 46, 144
Hooks, 13–16. *See also* Tandem hooks
  eyes, 14–15
Hrinko, Bill, 146
  Adams, 101
  Don's Delight, 96
  General MacArthur, 96
  Golden Witch, 97
  Greyhound, 97
  Magenta Maiden, 100
  Magog Special, 99
  Morning Glory, 98
  Orange Demon, 100
  Silver Darter Variation, 101
  West Branch Special, 99
  Wizard, 98

I

Ice-Out Special, 118
Indian Pond Special, 129
Indian Puddle, 132
Indian Summer, 94
Islander, 126

J

Jim Warner Special, 130
Jock Scott Bucktail, 110
Jungle cock, 9, 18–19

K

Kennebago Muddler, 94
Kevlar thread, 17
Kim's Special, 107

L

Lac Ternay Special, 137
Lady Amherst pheasant, 7
Lady Doctor, 53–60
Libby, Arthur
  A.W.L., 105
  Green Wonder, 104
  Hazel, 103
  Libby's Cal, 106
  Lib's Smelt, 104
  Miss Sharon, 105
  Rain, 106

  Robin, 102
  Senator Muskie, 103
Libby's Cal, 106
Libby's Flies, 103-106
  Lib's Smelt, 104
Limerick hook bends, 15
Llama Hair "Brown Julie," 115
Llama Hair Chapman's Smelt, 119
Looped-eye hooks, 14–15

M

McKusick, Ron, 146
  Barred Orange Pink Lady, 138
  Governor Barrows, 137
  Lac Ternay Special, 137
  Moosehead Smelt-Fall, 136
  Moosehead Smelt-Spring, 135
  Moosehead Smelt-Summer, 136
Magenta Maiden, 100
Magog Special, 99
Maisey, Grahame, 15
Mann, Charlie, 146
  Blueback, 108
  Champlain Jane, 109
  Jock Scott Bucktail, 110
  Miller's Special, 109
Marabou (marabou streamers), 10, 19
  The Ballou Special, 10, 63–67
Martinek, Mike, Jr., 15, 30, 146
  Brave American, 130
  Chartreuse Ghost, 125
  Dun Wanderer, 128
  Electric Perch, 127
  Fryes Leap, 126
  Gray Eye, 124
  Indian Pond Special, 129
  Islander, 126
  Jim Warner Special, 130
  Midnight Sun, 128
  Mike's Red Ghost Special, 125
  Orange Dragon, 127
  Winni Pinni, 129
Materials, 13–20. *See also* specific
  materials
  purveyors of, 144
Merrymeeting Special, 131
Midnight Blue Ghost, 117
Midnight Sun, 128
Mike's Red Ghost Special, 125
Miller's Special, 109
Miss Sharon, 105
Monocord thread, 17
Moosehead Smelt-Fall, 136

Moosehead Smelt-Spring, 135
Moosehead Smelt-Summer, 136
Morning Glory, 98
Ms. Bushaw, The, 114
Muddler Minnow, 81–85
Muzeroll, Ed "Muzzy," 134, 146
  The Enticer, 135
Mylar tinsel, 17–18

N

Nelson, Roland, 35
Northridge, Henry, 147
  Guides Special, 131
  Merrymeeting Special, 131

O

Oatman, Lew, 134
One-Eyed Poacher, 110
Orange Demon, 100
Orange Dragon, 127
Orange Tiger, 2
Oval tinsel, 18

P

Pavlik, The, 124
Percy Tackle Company, 53
Pink Beauty, 89
Polar-bear hair, 20
Purple Haze, 121

Q

Quebec Whore, 92
Queen of the Lake, 121

R

Rain, 106
Rangeley Streamer hooks, 15
Red Dog, The, 113
Red Ghost Special, 125
Red Gray Ghost, 120
Ring-eye hooks, 14, 15
Ring-necked pheasant, 6
Robin, 102

S

Santiam Sunrise, 95
Scoville, G. S. "Stack," Jr., 95, 102,
  138–143, 147
  Allie's Delight, 139
  Allie's Favorite, 138
  America, 141

Artula, 139
Blue Devil, 140
Blue Dragon, 140
Canary, 141
Canary-Custom, 142
Carrie's Favorite, 95
Carrie's Special, 142
Casablanca, 143
Charles E. Wheeler, 143
Chief, 102
Senator Muskie, 103
Shang's Favorite, 49–51
Shang's Special, 134
Sheep's hair, 20
Shelburne Bay Sunset, 113
Shoulders, 10
Shushan Postmaster, 133
Silk flosses, 17
Silk threads, 16
Silver Darter Variation, 101
Silver pheasant, 4, 24
Smelt (smelt flies), 1–2. *See also*
   specific flies
Smith, Monte, 147
   Indian Summer, 94
   Santiam Sunrise, 95
Spirit of '76, 117
Sproat hook bends, 15
Stevens, Carrie, 13, 22–24, 32,
   45–55, 88–92, 95–98, 138–139,
   141–143
Stickney, Joseph, 53
Streamer components
   bellies, 3
   bodies, 3, 17–18
   ribs, 3
   tags, 3
   tails, 3
   topping, 10
   throats, 3
   underwings, 3
   wings, 3, 18–19
Stretch-nylon floss, 17
Supervisor, 122
Suppliers, 144
Synthetic hairs, 20, 69

T

Talleur, Dick, 147
   Baby Brook Trout, 134
   Golden Darter, 133
   Shushan Postmaster, 133
Tandem hooks, 15–16, 17

Tandem-hook streamers, 1, 41–51
   The Blue Sapphire, 41–44
   Shang's Favorite, 49–51
   The Tomahawk, 45–48
Threads, 16–17
Thunder Creek, 15, 75–79
Tiers. *See also* specific tiers
   featured, 145–47
Tinsels, 17–18
Tomah Joe, 112
Tomahawk, The, 45–48
Trolling, tandem hooks for, 1, 15–16,
   41. *See also* Tandem-hook streamers
Tube Fly Tying Tool, 45–46
Tube Tandem-Hook Streamer, 45–48

U

Upham, Bob, 147
   Golden Head, 111
   Grand Laker, 111
   One-Eyed Poacher, 110
   Tomah Joe, 112
   Wholly Ghost, 112

W

West Branch Special, 99
West Canada, 132
White Ghost, 93
Whiting, Tom, 18
Whiting Farms, 18
Wholly Ghost, 112
Winni Pinni, 129
Witch, 89
Wizard, 98
Wolf, Gray, 147
   Brown Shadow, 116
   Candy's Smelt, 116
   Coral Smelt, 115
   D.K. Special, 119
   Doctor's Wife, 118
   Flaming Beauty, 120
   Ice-Out Special, 118
   Llama Hair "Brown Julie," 115
   Llama Hair Chapman's Smelt, 119
   Midnight Blue Ghost, 117
   Orange Tiger, 2
   Purple Haze, 121
   Queen of the Lake, 121
   Red Gray Ghost, 120
   Spirit of '76, 117
Wolfer, Ed, 147

Black Max, 108
The Gold Wonder, 107
Kim's Special, 107